WINDS *of* HEAVEN,
STUFF *of* EARTH

WINDS *of* HEAVEN, STUFF *of* EARTH

Spiritual Conversations Inspired by the Life & Lyrics of

RICH MULLINS

ANDREW GREER

and **RANDY COX**

WORTHY®
Inspired

The stuff of earth competes for the allegiance
I owe only to the Giver of all good things.

RICH MULLINS & STEVE CUDWORTH[1]

Published by Worthy Inspired, an imprint of Worthy Publishing Group, a division of Worthy Media, Inc., One Franklin Park, 6100 Tower Circle, Suite 210, Franklin, TN 37067.

WORTHY is a registered trademark of Worthy Media, Inc.

Helping people experience the heart of God

eBook available wherever digital books are sold.

Library of Congress Control Number: 2017946599

For foreign and subsidiary rights, contact rights@worthypublishing.com

ISBN: 978-1-68397-040-8

Interior Layout: Bart Dawson
Cover Design: Melissa Reagan
Cover Photo: Ben Pearson

Printed in the United States of America
17 18 19 20 21 LBM 9 8 7 6 5 4 3 2

CONTENTS

PART 3: TROUBADOUR

FOREWORD

Rich Mullins introduced me to an experience with God in the context of music that I had never known.

In 1981, I was attending college at Vanderbilt University in Nashville, Tennessee. A cassette tape of a song Rich had written landed on a desk at my management company. During a meeting with the team, I remember sitting around a Formica-top conference table, listening to songs I might record for a new album, when Rich's song started playing. By the end of "Sing Your Praise to the Lord," I was standing *on* that conference table, arms up in the air, whooping and hollering. I have been moved by a lot of songs, but when that song reached its iconic release point, I was levitating.

I ended up recording "Sing Your Praise to the Lord" on *Age to Age*. That was my first introduction to Rich. I think Rich and I both spent way too much time in our heads—I still do—so our friendship just clicked. He was disarmingly honest about his life and the things that he struggled with, and he came at things from a different angle, a different perspective. Many times in our conversations I would think, *I hadn't thought about it that way.* He made lofty ideas about God so earthy. He humanized God. He humanized Jesus for me.

Rich didn't waste any time trying to be good, or at least trying to appear good. There's a little bit of good and bad in every one of us. But what Rich wanted to know, what we all want to know, is that we are loved.

For love to make the difference in any of our lives, much less in the world, we have to learn to receive it for ourselves. That learning is not a one-time thing, it is a daily thing, and it is in light of and in spite of all the things we grind on in our heads—all the chatter, all the old data that we allow to play over and over. Until we get quiet enough and still enough to receive love, or rather, *when* we get still and receive it, along with the experience of receiving love comes the absolute awareness that we are all connected equally to love. Equally. Then it makes sense when Jesus says, "If you have done it to the least of these, you have done it to me."[2]

We have made our wild, unique, overwhelming relationship with our Maker into a study. We go to Sunday school. Maybe we get a master's degree in theology. Rich was very smart, but he blew in the face of all that. The reality of a relationship with God is something completely different, and "other," and untouched by the study of God. While I love reading and studying the Bible and believe it is a life-giving pursuit of its own, it is not required for a relationship with Him. That's how Rich introduced people to God. He was always saying, *Here He is. Just open your eyes. He's right there. Give in. Lean in. Fall into Jesus.*

This is how he lived his life, and he made the rest of us curious.

The wind blows all around us as if it has a will of its own; we feel and hear it, but we do not understand where it has come from or where it will end up. Life in the Spirit is as if it were the wind of God.

JOHN 3:8

AMY GRANT
Nashville, Tennessee
March 2017

I am thinking now of old Moses: sitting on a mountain—sitting with God. I am thinking of the lump in his throat, that weary ache in his heart, that nearly bitter longing sweetened by the company of God. . . .

Of God, on whose breast old Moses lays His head like John the beloved would lay his on the Christ's. And God sits there quietly with Moses, for Moses, and lets His little man cry out his last moments of life.

And then God—the great eternal God—takes Moses's thin-worn, threadbare little body into His hands—hands into whose breath marked off the heavens—and with these enormous and enormously gentle hands, God folds Moses's pale, lifeless arms across his chest for burial.

I don't know if God wept at Moses's funeral. I don't know if He cried when He killed the first of His creatures, to take its skins to clothe this man's earliest ancestors. I don't know who will bury me. . . .

But I look back over the moments of my life and see the hands that carried Moses to his grave lifting me out of mine. In remembering, I go back to these places where God met me and I met Him again and I lay my head on His breast, and He shows me the land beyond the Jordan and I suck into my lungs the fragrance of His breath, the power of His presence.

Rich Mullins[3]

The Finish Line   by Richard Mullins

See him there digging in for a jump on time
muscles tense   only one thing on his mind
with the seconds ticking — giving him the sign
for the race to start — it's here to the finish line

———————— every movement has to count
he's thrown aside every weight that would slow him down
see the gains he's making - the distance he's left behind
moving on   to the finish line

‡ I've got to run   cause I know there's glory
                         at the finish for me
                         Lord, I just can't stand in place
so I've got to run   feel my strides lengthen
                         I run in Your strength and I
                         know You'll bring me to the end
                         to which You called me in your grace

Lord, You're showing me the way the eagles fly
the end is near — no time to look aside
the world is calling but I know it's time
to throw it off and get to the finish line

                         (repeat chorus)

INTRODUCTION

Richard Wayne Mullins died September 19, 1997. He was one month shy of his forty-second birthday. A tragic auto accident along Illinois Interstate 39 took his life and abruptly ended a provocative musical career. The prophetic poet had been silenced. We felt the void and we grieved our loss.

Like many culture influences whose lives are cut short, seemingly overnight Rich Mullins's life and work became a focal point of a tribe of followers seeking authentic communion within the conversations he perpetuated. Rich's conversations were centered by Jesus's practices and heaven's perspectives rather than man-made religions and church-created expectations. And because he began his conversations with music, they felt safer.

Growing up in a Baptist congregation on the rural eastern edge of West Texas, I knew the poetry of his music. Songs like "Awesome God," "Sometimes by Step," and "Hold Me Jesus"—forerunners of the modern worship music movement—were staples on our radios, in our homes, and worship services. Rich's unparalleled songwriting prose housed the most tender prayers inside accessible melodic sensibilities. And it was within the musical breadth of *A Liturgy, a Legacy, and a Ragamuffin Band* that I first learned honest-to-God songwriting was not exclusive to music in the mainstream, but was also available to spiritual seekers inside the church.

But it wasn't Rich's legend, his musicality, or even his lyrics that got to me. It was Rich himself who moved me.

He asked lots of questions. Whether in a discourse with close friends or fellow artists, with concert audiences, or within the confines of a narrow music industry, Rich punctuated his exchanges with question marks. He urged conversations forward through illustrations of his own vulnerable search for God and inner peace—for some permanent solution to this so obviously temporal human condition.

He was unafraid and unashamed to love people, especially those lingering on the outskirts of society, popularity, and success. His generous lifestyle and provocative dialogue bolstered the notion that God loves us "as we are, not as we should be"—as phrased by his beloved confidant, Brennan Manning.

He was indifferent to the rules of an impersonal religion and unimpressed by America's twentieth-century corporate church concoctions. Yet he remained ensconced in Scripture, and he was captivated by the relational power of communion.

In his persistent search for that seemingly impossible but Jesus-like balance of truth and grace, Rich was absolutely and totally enamored by eternal matters. His incessant hunt for eternity that ensued has caused more than one of his close companions to wonder if his tragic auto accident, now twenty years since, was a result of this fiery urge to embody the fullness of forever as soon as was earthly possible.

He was truly haunted by *home*.

Still, twenty years after his unexpected death, it remains a mystery as to how Rich's honest songwriting would have fared inside an industry narrowed by the confines of "modern worship" music's commercialism. But regardless of the industry's fashions and trends, the inspiration of his lyrics and his life continue to surge through the lives and work of many voices who are influencing culture today. My hope is that this book has offered a gracious space for some of those people to share their experiences of faith and doubt as inspired by Rich's life—a life full of faith and doubt.

More than a tribute to his music, or a biography of his life, this discourse has been drafted for those of us who, like Rich, courageously maneuver through the enigma of faith in the hopes of surrendering to Jesus, one day, completely.

I never expected to connect so deeply with the person

of Rich. And I suspect, after perusing these pages, you might relate to him too. Consider these conversations, from Rich . . . for you.

In the ragamuffin spirit,
Andrew Greer
Franklin, Tennessee
March 2017

Rich Mullins with the Amy Grant Unguarded Encore Tour, 1986.

Top: Rich's house in Bellsburg, Tennessee, formerly served as the parsonage for this church, Bethel Methodist. *Bottom:* The church's doors were always open and Rich would play this piano and sing hymns with his guests.

LOVE ALONE

The Gospel of Belonging

And while reasons may be found within His love, no reason would be able to contain His love. . . . It is possible that the evidence of His divinity lies in that love—that in light of love, miracles seem sort of unremarkable. If God can love me, the rest will follow.

RICH MULLINS[1]

The Amy Grant Unguarded Encore Tour, 1986.

Love Alone

The song was broken on the silence.
The day fell deep into the shadows.
Torn from His heart the music echoed,
I love you.

The prayer went out and then the candle.
The grave was sealed, the promise sleeping,
And through the dark the quiet whispered,
I love you.

And broader still than time and space,
His love alone, through heaven's grace,
One sacrifice for every life.
Our sin atoned
By love alone

The stone was moved and eyes were opened
And joy came walking from the sadness.
Now in our hearts still His voice lingers.
I love you. . . .

Unpublished lyrics by Rich Mullins, Phil Naish,
and Lowell Alexander[2]

Rich on the road with good friends David McCracken and Marita Meinerts Albinson, 1990.

Part 1

INTRODUCTION

The more I uncover about Rich Mullins's interior life, the more I connect to the tenacious tension he let us see between his mind, heart, and soul in the knowing about God's love, believing in God's love, and, ultimately, receiving God's love. Perhaps his relentless struggle to care for and love himself decently compelled him to care for and love others wholly.

He seemed to have an almost unrelieved longing to be invited, to be included. Long before "inclusivity" became a culturally correct term, Rich embodied it. The unconditional character of his love, the equality (and therefore *quality*) of his acceptance for all people, and his genuine service to his neighbors (especially for those who were poor and broken—which in some way defines us all), compelled others to participate in his conversation—some to criticize, some to confirm, but drawn in nonetheless.

Compelled by compassion, Rich limited his salary to an "everyman's wage" so that he could share his financial good fortune with his "Ragamuffin" musical family and with organizations and individuals who invested in partnering with the disenfranchised and those relegated to the fringes of society. During the last few years of his life, he fashioned his professional life to provide the infrastructure for his growing kinship with the Navajo and his fervor for teaching music to children in the reservation schools.

Very practically, Rich's life was inspired by love, and by love alone

The origin of love begins with the Creator's own tender pronouncement: "God looked over everything he had made; it was so good, so very good!" Genesis 1:31 (MSG). This inborn truth—that He created us and created us well—elevates our existence from some scientific experiment conjured up by a distant deity to purposeful people instilled with the essence of eternity by the imagination of a Creator whose perfect presence we reflect. To risk scattering His image across the cosmos via free-willed creatures . . . He must be crazy. Or, *in love.*

Rich understood *the Fall* is in us all and he was keenly aware of his own transgressions. But he had a way of turning our focus from the despair of sin to the hope of Jesus, who is persistently wooing us back to the table of grace through love. He insisted that with all of our darkness, not in spite of it, we belong in the company of God's light. Or more succinctly, we are loved by God, therefore we belong.

Through Rich's life and songs, he perpetuated this dialogue that began when God created you and me, and created us "so very good." Love, as it was in the beginning . . .

A barefooted Rich with his dog, Curry, on the front porch of his home in Bellsburg, Tennessee.

CHAPTER 1

BARE

Cindy Morgan

Humility is not thinking less of yourself:
it is thinking of yourself less.

C. S. LEWIS

He was barefoot.

The meeting ground between something sacred and something raw and human is written throughout the pages of history.

God speaks to Moses through a burning bush: "Take off your sandals, for the place where you are standing is holy ground" (Exodus 3:5 NIV). Adam and Eve, covered in fig leaves in the garden, when God asks, "Who told you that you were naked?" (Genesis 3:11 NIV). Jesus hanging on the cross, depicted with only a loincloth over His battered figure, His bloody feet pierced by a large nail.

Leading up to His crucifixion, I wonder if Jesus was stripped of His sandals, wilting under the weight of the beam of wood that would become His cross as He carried it down the narrow street of the "Via Dolorosa" (which translated means the "Painful Way"), His bare feet digging into sharp rocks and gravel with each agonizing step.

Bare.

It is the state in which we arrive to life, without any protection or disguise to cover our nakedness, our shame, who we are in our most raw and vulnerable form. We learn to present ourselves, to put our best foot forward. We wear our finest clothes, our most stylish statement, hiding what truly is for fear of falling short. We are afraid there isn't enough grace to cover our sin, so we desperately try to cover it up.

The last time I saw Rich Mullins we were performing an event—strangely enough, called "The Spectacular"— at Nashville's historic Ryman Auditorium. The concert was hosted during the week of the Dove Awards, Gospel music's annual awards show, as a kind of holy spectacle showcasing Christian music's brightest talent. I had been a part of the event for many years, but that year—that night—it would be different.

From the moment Rich stepped onto the stage, the atmosphere changed in that old church. While all of the rest of us donned our most expensive clothes, Rich walked out wearing a crumpled black T-shirt and jeans faded not from an artificial processing to make them look just so, but faded from real wear and real tear. His hair hung down in an unkempt, unintentional bob, the result of not giving much thought to a haircut. Then I looked down and saw the thing that made me the most surprised . . .

No shoes.

His brown bare feet padded across the wood floor of the Ryman stage, and as he sat down at a nine-foot Steinway piano, I imagined him pressing down the sustain pedal, how it must have been cold and slippery. But it didn't faze Rich in the slightest. He began to play "Our God Is an Awesome God." The air in the auditorium was electrified by his voice and his musicianship. By his vulnerability, his inability to care what others thought, his rawness before God and before us. It is a moment I will never forget.

At the end of the song, the audience erupted with a standing ovation, begging Rich for another song. He looked at the crowd in a sort of bewilderment and walked off the stage, never to return. I wonder if Rich was thinking that we had missed the whole point of the song . . . "Our God is an awesome God," not "Rich is an awesome artist."

God is the point of our existence, not success, or fame, or looking the part, or covering up that which is unseemly or sinful or embarrassing.

Let us lay bare that which we are, the things we struggle with, all that we cannot hide anyway, and place them at the holy, bare feet of Jesus, or we may never experience the true grace and mercy of an awesome and loving God. Where the struggler meets the sacred. Where our humanity meets holiness.

Nothing in all creation is hidden from God's sight. Everything is uncovered and laid bare before the eyes of him to whom we must give account.

HEBREWS 4:13 NIV

CHAPTER 2

FLAWS AND ALL

*Be kind, for everyone you meet
is fighting a hard battle.*
IAN MACLAREN

This affective, widely cited quote is most commonly attributed to Ian MacLaren, the pen name for nineteenth-century Scottish author and theologian Reverend John Watson. Though the phraseology is charming, the admonition within is penetrating.

We all carry baggage, don't we? Some of us are weighted down with particularly dense issues. Rich certainly was. We press through difficult relationships, commit ourselves to recovery from addictions, and fight against low self-esteem and low-grade depressions. Life requires much of many of us, and so we discipline our lives, attempting to work through and around all that we lug mentally, emotionally, and spiritually. And yet, these issues persist in possessing our attention and affection.

Though the details of our lives storybook very differently, at some point, we all understand hardship.

In becoming aware of our shortcomings, we often become critical of ourselves, and of others. But when we allow our hearts to be purged of what feels temporarily good by what is eternally best, we become more gracious to ourselves, and to others. And grace makes the world go 'round.

We will never fully know what it cost the person sitting next to us on Sunday to slip out of bed, slide into that pew, and pray that prayer. I would venture to say most of us don't know what it takes for any of us to get to the sanctuary. All the beds lain in. All the nitty-gritty we try to surrender but struggle to forfeit. We keep working for Jesus's attention, rather than simply accepting His friendship.

It's impossible for us to live blameless lives. But we can share our battle scars as an invitation to dive into the deep end of redemption—where fear is washed out by forgiveness, guilt is drowned by grace, and heartache is plunged beneath waves of healing, over and over again.

"Be kind, for everyone you meet is fighting a hard battle."

This is our story. This was Rich's song. Flaws and all.

Yet you have a few people in Sardis who have not soiled their clothes. They will walk with me, dressed in white, for they are worthy. The one who is victorious will, like them, be dressed in white. I will never blot out the name of that person from the book of life, but will acknowledge that name before my Father and his angels.

REVELATION 3:4–5 NIV

I am a Christian because I have seen the love of God lived out in the lives of people who know Him. The Word has become flesh and I have encountered God in the people who have manifested (in many "unreasonable" ways) His Presence; a Presence that is more than convincing—it is a Presence that is compelling.

RICH MULLINS

CHAPTER 3

THE RAGAMUFFIN TRUTH[3]

Brennan Manning

*Next to Jesus, maybe all the heavens and the hills
of the earth, all the music and works of art, all the rainbows
and wines and burning bushes and boars seem like
tiny tokens—great as they are—and maybe the issue is not
so much about how and through what God swears His love,
as it is about whether or not God does love.*

RICH MULLINS

I consider meeting Rich Mullins one of the most truthful times in my life. We met the first time in Colorado Springs. I was out there doing a short, three-day preaching mission and Rich was also visiting. He asked me [if he] could do an interview. Rich talked about the grace of God rather than personal performance, and that was a track I was locked into—personal performance, which, by the way, never works.

If you examine the content of his writing, you have so many frequent references to the love of God in Christ Jesus that it seems to overshadow everything else. That's the impression I got. He wrote with utter simplicity and candor about his own brokenness.

Rich's candor and brutal honesty . . . opened the door to all kinds of questions for me. The honesty, when he was talking about his own life, was so refreshing. He was not ashamed to talk about anything—his successes, his failures, and there was nothing out of bounds.

Suppose you came to the conviction of the Holy Spirit that the most important value in life was letting yourself be loved by God? Talk about a radical transformation, a total absence of low self-esteem . . . not boastful. [That's how Rich was.] I think you know when you meet somebody who is absolutely convinced of the love of God. And when they're not, they are mouthing the pious phrases and it's all basically fraud. They haven't laid hold of the depth of the reality of God's love.

Rich spent a lot of time in solitude, which I believe is indispensable for anyone who would come to grips with the love of God. [Solitude is] a prayer of listening—letting yourself be loved by God. As outrageous as it may seem, [it is admitting] that God really has a thing for me. . . . No matter what comes down, He can't stop loving you. When that becomes the hard right truth of your existence, [you] let God be God.

In my limited experiences of the real lovers of God, [they] are always solitary men and women. They have a sheer delight in being alone with God because they are not waiting for Him to remind them of their latest hang-ups. He knows all about that better than they do.

The love of God is not a nice theory; it's a pious reality, but it so marks your day. What else matters? To be loved by God—to me, that's the heart of Christianity, letting myself be loved, in spite of all the powerful evidence to the contrary. Letting God be God.

We have experienced and we have entrusted our lives to the love of God in us.

God is love. Anyone who lives faithfully in love also lives faithfully in God, and God lives in him. This love is fulfilled with us, so that on the day of judgment we have confidence based on our identification with Jesus in this world. Love will never invoke fear. Perfect love expels fear, particularly the fear of punishment. The one who fears punishment has not been completed through love.

1 JOHN 4:16–18

R MULLINS

THE HATCHING OF A HEART

THE NIGHT WAS COLD & MY HEART WAS HIDDEN VERY SAFELY IN A SHELL
& I KNEW SOMEHOW I'D HAVE TO RUN THAT RISK — HAVE TO OPEN UP MYSELF
YOU SAID "LOOK AT THE STARS ON THE FACE OF THE SKY — THEY'RE THE SAME ONES ABRAHAM SAW
COME UNDER MY WINGS I WILL MAKE YOU SHINE GIVE YOU STRENGTH ENOUGH TO LOVE"

1 — I'M GETTING STRONG ENOUGH
YOU HELPED ME CHIP MY WAY OUT HELPED ME OPEN MYSELF UP

SO FOR THE SNOW THAT COMES WITH WINTER FOR THE GROWTH THAT COMES WITH PAIN
FOR THE JOKE I CAN'T REMEMBER ALTHO THE LAUGHTER LONG REMAINS
FOR THE FAITH THAT BROUGHT TO FINISH ALL I DOUBTED AT THE START
LORD, I GIVE YOU PRAISE FOR ALL THAT MAKES FOR THE HATCHING OF A HEART

WELL, MY FACE WAS SMOOTH & FEATURELESS JUST LIKE AN EGG
& IF I WAS MOVED YOU WOULD NEVER GUESS IT BY THE LOOK UPON MY FACE
BUT YOU SAID "MAN LOOKS WITHOUT BUT I LOOK WITHIN I CAN SEE THE LOVE YOU HIDE
IT'S A MATTER OF DOUBT IT'S A SYMPTOM OF SIN IT'S A PROBLEM OF TOO MUCH PRIDE"

SO I — I'M OPENING UP WIDE
WET FEATHERS FOLD OUT FROM BENEATH ME & YOU'RE TEACHING ME TO FLY

SO FOR THE WARMTH THAT COMES WITH FRIENDSHIP FOR THE STRENGTH THAT COMES WITH HOPE
FOR THE LOVE TIME CAN'T DIMINISH & FOR THE TIME LOVE TAKES TO GROW
FOR THE MOONLIGHT ON THE RIVER FOR THE BRIGHT & MORNING STAR
LORD, I GIVE YOU PRAISE FOR ALL THAT MAKES FOR THE HATCHING OF A HEART

CHAPTER 4

REFLECTIONS ON RICH

David McCracken

---

*The joy of Christian life is that those aches, those needs,
that emptiness that we are going to encounter
because we are human is ultimately met in Christ.
And that everything that we try to fill it
with that is not Christ will never really fill it.*

RICH MULLINS

"Don't you ever get tired of being . . . *perfect?*" he asked.

"Huh?" I muttered, completely oblivious as to where this conversation was headed.

With a clarity that was a little too close for my comfort, he repeated, "Don't you ever get tired of pretending like everything in your life is fine, David?"

Wait a minute. Three seconds ago I thought this conversation was going to be about *him*. Whiplashed into full engagement, I said, "What are you talking about? You know my life isn't perfect."

"Yes, I do, but have you ever thought about the beauty you might experience if you were brave enough to share the broken parts of yourself with anyone else?"

I met Rich when I was a naïve college kid interning at the record label where he had recently signed a deal. And for the next twelve years we navigated life together. I became his champion at a time when he desperately needed one, and he certainly was mine. I had never experienced a friendship like his before. At that moment, I wasn't sure that I wanted one that would dare to call my lifelong bluff. In a way that only a true friend could, he used this conversation to lovingly guide me toward seeing a counselor for the first time.

After politely listening to the story of my life up to that point, my new counselor said it sounded like I had lived a perfectly perfect life and she wasn't sure that I needed God—much less her insight. She thought I should try living apart from a relationship with God so that I could really discover whether or not my need for Him was real. I balked at her challenge. With all I could muster of my own strength, I clung for years to my idea of what a relationship with God looks like as I continued to live my very best, "perfect" life.

And then Rich died.

I was not even close to being equipped to face the pain of that loss. And so I didn't.

Ten years later, I finally began to allow myself to fully experience the depth of my grief. I did not do it perfectly. I felt that I had been cosmically sucker-punched by the loss of my most intimate friend, and I was paralyzed with fear that no one would ever know and love me as well as Rich had. So at the decade-old prodding of my counselor, I set out on a mission to find out if I really did need God—a mission that at first was utterly self-destructive.

In an effort to strip myself of the places where I found Him readily available, I abandoned a church community that would never have abandoned me and I pulled away from anyone who might offer some real hope. I started drinking. I lost fifty pounds in six weeks. Friends thought I was dying, and though I wasn't exactly trying to kill myself, for eighteen months I tested God to see if He had any interest at all in saving me—to see if He thought I was worth saving. After ignoring several of His creative attempts to get my attention, my reckless behavior resulted in my involvement in a serious car accident. I broke bones from head to toe, smashed my nose, busted my eye socket, endured a fractured wrist and elbow, and shattered my ankle. Now a plethora of permanent plates and screws are a daily reminder of what happens when you abandon real hope.

What I remember most while recuperating is that every time I opened my eyes there was an outrageously and beautifully diverse group of saints at my bedside. As I was wheeled away for surgery to repair my body, I recall the beloved friends who laid hands on me, praying for the healing of my soul . . . the holy hands and tender hearts of my softball teammates as they shaved my face and washed the dried blood from my hair . . . my relatives and my "chosen" family who continued to love and provide constant care for me long after doctors had gathered and healed my broken pieces. Every one of the loved ones who surrounded me were an example of Rich's challenge to allow myself to be known and loved, not in spite of, but because of my brokenness.

There are days when it is still brutally painful to experience moments of recognition of Rich. But sometimes, even in those moments, the skies split and I discover evidence of heaven—when I find glimpses of him in nature, when I see pieces of him in art, and as I encounter him in the lives of my fellow ragamuffins. I still weep when I read that Jonathan loved David "as his own soul."[4] But it is in experiencing Rich's words where I find myself most, and isn't that the power, and the beauty, and the mystery of his music—finding parts of ourselves hidden in the lines of his poetry?

And for the snow that comes with winter,
For the growth that comes from pain,
For the joke I can't remember,
Although the laughter long remains,
For the faith that brought to finish
All I doubted at the start,
Lord, I give You praise for all that makes—
For the hatching of a heart. . . .

RICH MULLINS, "THE HATCHING OF A HEART"[5]

Twenty years later, I can barely read these words without them breaking my heart and driving me to my knees. But his music has always had that power—to break and to humble me—and I suppose that isn't such a bad place to be after all.

We go, "Wow, will I ever stop hurting?" My answer is, "Don't worry about hurting. Realize this is how badly God wants you." That hurt you are feeling, that emptiness you are feeling, maybe that's what it feels to be called by God. So don't try to fill it. Don't try to quiet it. Ask God to give you the courage to face that and walk through that to Him.

RICH MULLINS [6]

CHAPTER 5

SKIN ON SKIN

*If you took the whole Bible, and you shook it around
and melted it down and said, "What is the essence
of what this whole thing is saying?" I think it would
just be that God loves you very much.
That God in fact is crazy about you.*

RICH MULLINS[7]

Stories about Rich's vagabond lifestyle abound. His long-time producer and friend, Reed Arvin, recalls one such story from the height of Rich's career successes:

"Once, I met Rich for an early morning meeting at our record company. Rich had come in from Wichita. I found him standing alone by his suitcase in the parking lot.

'Where's your car?' I asked.

'Didn't drive.'

'So, what, you took a cab from the airport?'

'Didn't fly. I hitchhiked.'

It had taken him three days. He'd been dropped off at a breakfast place, was fed, and then walked to the label, suitcase in tow."

I wonder if Rich's "risky" behavior was an attempt—amid chart-topping radio singles, sold out shows, and substantial record sales—to keep his feet on the ground. As methods of communication advanced expeditionally, I wonder if Rich was making a decided effort to connect to others through these down-to-earth experiences and, through them, found a way to relate more closely with God.

We are all looking for real connection. More than ever before in human history, we are connected to each other. Through the phenomenal technological advancements of the last century—even the last twenty years—we can now relate to each other on various levels, in various ways, instantly. Whether we take the time to be cognizant of the implications of the Digital Age or not, the ability to communicate from anywhere, about anything, in real time, is quite awesome.

It's also hairy.

By sharing and airing the details of our dirty laundry via the social circles of the interweb, we create the perception of transparency while in actuality we stuff the nitty-gritty of our day-to-day realities below our cyberspace chitter-chatter. This around-the-clock social networking creates an allusion of connectivity, but it is a shallow invitation for followers—not friends—to feed into our Information Age inner circle. I call this "one-way communion." Some call it narcissism. You pick. I have been guilty of both.

This surface-deep interaction is not a substitute for the value (and necessity) of *face time relationships* (a common phrase long before Apple coined it as an iPhone Application). Until we shoulder up with our neighbors, we cannot really know one another. And until we know one another, we cannot learn from each other. And only when we are open and ready to learn from each other will we truly love one another.

Rich didn't just communicate with people, he lived among them. He invited them into his spaces, he rode with them in cars, and he lived with them skin on skin in their world.

Perhaps this is why the Incarnation is so integral to our faith, to our beliefs, and to our living for now—and forever. If God is too big, too distant, or too aloof, if He only hovers over us but doesn't dwell within us, how are we more than dust particles randomly compiled into existence? We keep craning our necks around misused Scriptures and complicated theology to catch some real-time encounter with our Creator, to find out if He really knows what it is like to wear this skin and embody these bones. We keep wondering if we are more than some Eden experiment gone awry.

This must be why God introduced us to Jesus, because if He gets it—if He understands pain, and confusion, and doubt, and grief, and the toil of work—if he gets *us*, everything changes.

"Jesus did not come to change the mind of God about humanity. Jesus came to change the mind of humanity about God," wrote Richard Rohr.

Without this skin on skin relationship with God, how could we truly know Him? And if we don't know Him, how can we learn from Him? And if we aren't open and ready to learn from Him, how will we discover the most profound truth of all time . . . God loves you and me?

There are many things in the Christian faith that are hard to get a handle on, and one of the things that I struggle the hardest with is believing that God really loves me. It's too good to believe, but it's true. Whether I can believe it or not.

RICH MULLINS

CHAPTER 6

RADICAL LOVE

Sarah Hart

Love is something God generates—
it looks very much like Him.

<small>RICH MULLINS</small>

One of my dearest friends said this to me once: "Love is hard, because love requires time." I have burned that into my heart. As a mom, there is nothing—*nothing*—that my children crave more than time with me. Just time.

In light of our overworked, hyper-individualistic, technological, noise-filled lives, it is truly revolutionary to turn off our phones, stop working, sit down with someone, and say, "I am listening. I am paying attention. I am here." Love requires shutting down our desires for ourselves— our need to keep busy, our constant filling the void— to truly give of our time to another.

Love has always been difficult, but I feel the burden of it being more arduous than ever before. In our current social climate, it seems foolish, and stands against our reason, to be kind, accepting, helpful, and forgiving. Our society, again, with its current bent toward hyper-individualism, prompts us to succeed! To live large! To say, "My political position is right! My religion is better than yours!" These are the cries of a culture of people that have become far too inwardly focused.

To buy into these cultural messages, that is where true foolishness lies. As Thomas Merton said, "The beginning of love is the will to let those we love be perfectly themselves, the resolution not to twist them to fit our own image."

Jesus had a gentle way of turning attention away from Himself in order to impress upon others that they were loved, important, and heard. He never stayed in one place for long, never soaked up the glory or stuck around for accolades—He merely gave of Himself for the sake of another and moved on. Of course, we will never master this as Jesus did, but that should not deter us from trying. It is something Rich Mullins spent his life trying to do.

I believe this message of love becomes more crucial as we grow further from the historical time in which Jesus actually walked here on earth. The challenge with the growing distractions of each new generation is to make time for others by offering our very best (not our most convenient) time and talent—to truly give without expectation of receiving. When we give of ourselves in this way, we understand what Christ was trying to impress upon us—that all are welcome, all are beloved, and all belong.

My loved ones, let us devote ourselves to loving one another. Love comes straight from God, and everyone who loves is born of God and truly knows God.

1 JOHN 4:7

To be chosen as the Beloved of God is something radically different. Instead of excluding others, it includes others. Instead of rejecting others as less valuable, it accepts others in their own uniqueness. It is not a competitive, but a compassionate choice. Our minds have great difficulty in coming to grips with such a reality. Maybe our minds will never understand it. Perhaps it is only our hearts that can accomplish this.

HENRI NOUWEN

CHAPTER 7

TRIBE AND TONGUE

*I think part of holiness is having
right relationships with people.*

RICH MULLINS

In many ways, music was Rich's first language. His ability to speak candidly with his audience about whatever was running around in his mind or weighing on his heart was the result of music. The melodious medium offered him the space to say what he felt while offering listeners the grace to receive it without offense (well, most of the time).

Music facilitates the conversations we often can't find the courage to begin with words alone.

Music and the divine are so intertwined that, no matter the situation, when the strains of music are involved, the Spirit of God is hovering close. Perhaps this is why Rich's listeners felt so connected with Rich, because through music, he was helping them start a conversation with God.

But spiritual songs often include conversations more influenced by a country or region's history and heritage than a specific religion or belief system. Here in the United States, tunes like "Wade in the Water," "His Eye Is on the Sparrow," and "Amazing Grace" are as much accepted by mainstream culture as they are affirmed in the Church. The long progress of the African-American community has been marked by sacred hymns—or "spirituals"—inspired as much by a drive for social shifts and fights for equality as a search for God.

Last year, with my parlor guitar in tow, I traipsed across Bulgaria to perform songs from a wide catalog of sources—everything from country, to folk, to pop, and gospel—in an effort to initiate conversations about life, both the physical and the spiritual realm, with folks from taverns to churches, to neighborhoods and schools. To keep my performance near the place where music— and subsequently God—first took hold of my heart, I would end each set list with a hymn.

One evening, at the conclusion of the concert, I asked the audience if they knew an old hymn, "How Great Thou Art." Before that particular concert, a local college student explained that concealed under the wooden floor of the church where I would be performing was a pool once used to baptize followers of Jesus under the cover of dark, while Bulgaria slogged under the control of Communism. Behind the Iron Curtain of the country's former government, citizens caught attending church would be outed and ostracized for their faith. So as I started to sing the first verse, "*O Lord my God / When I in awesome wonder,*" I was not unaffected by the echoes of persecution reverberating just beneath my feet, or what a musical expression of faith like the one we were sharing at that moment in the public square once cost Bulgarians.

Gradually, as the weight of remembrance was distributed through the room, each audience member in their native tongue—some Bulgarian, some English—stood to their feet in an impromptu singing ovation to our great Redeemer and Friend: *"Then sings my soul, my Savior God to Thee / How great Thou art, how great Thou art."* And as our cultures began to comingle under the beautiful communion of music, I remembered that even though we are foreign by definition, we are family in our hearts.

Our modern world way of relating can be completely backwards. We have become so mired in our opposing views, our dissimilarities, sometimes even in what we label as "diversity," that we fail to remember that we have all been created as a reflection of Him to be in *right relationship with people*. We are *all* invited to eat at His table—without exclusion.

So let's drop our defenses. Let go of our opinions. Unclinch those fists. Open our minds, expose our hearts, and turn our gazes to the heavens where the very goodness of God is reflected through every iota of the universe. Every last one of us, regardless of tribe or tongue, is a complex and beautiful creature created with eternal love, united under divine purpose, and made—from the beginning—part of one family.

If we carefully obey everything the Eternal our God has commanded us, then we'll be living as we should, in righteousness and in right relationship with Him.

DEUTERONOMY 6:25

CHAPTER 8

REFLECTIONS ON RICH

Lowell Alexander

Listen to your life. See it for the fathomless mystery it is.
In the boredom and pain of it, no less than
in the excitement and gladness: touch, taste,
smell your way to the holy and hidden heart of it,
because in the last analysis all moments
are key moments, and life itself is grace.

FREDERICK BUECHNER

Not long after Rich's record *Pictures in the Sky* had released, he and I were driving through Nashville, headed to a church where he was to perform that evening. As we were winding our way through a crowded traffic situation, a man in a rusty Toyota sped down the ramp, nearly side-swiping us. The man's face was next to the passenger side window of our car, so Rich and I both caught a front-seat look at the road rage offender.

He had a ruddy complexion and a tattered jacket pulled up around his neck. A cigarette dangled from his mouth like some old B-movie villain, and his recklessness caused panic on our little portion of the freeway. After the shock of almost being pummeled, we looked up, and the man was right in front of us.

My initial reaction was to follow him and beat him like a rented mule. Rich must have felt similarly. Amid the chaos, I looked over and saw the writer of "Sing Your Praise to the Lord" lean up on the dashboard, taunting the weathered driver who was now watching us through his rearview mirror.

Rich, with his first and second fingers positioned as if he were smoking, was pulling the invisible cigarette frantically to and from his mouth, mocking the reckless driver. Then, as the Toyota sped away, Rich sat back in his seat, and a quiet hung heavy for the next mile or so—until he spoke the words I will never forget. Out of the silence I heard Rich say, with that familiar Midwestern accent, "I know that was Jesus."

He sighed and looked so sad at that moment, as if he had failed a test from God Himself. As he stared out the window, he said it again, as if growing more disheartened, "I know that was Jesus." We sat in silence for the rest of the drive. In those few words, he had simply and profoundly summed up so much of the gospel. Rich knew he had failed to consider that man as Christ would have considered him. I also failed that day but took away a lifetime lesson—Rich's words showed me a person serious about sculpting away the ugly edges of his life until only a work of art, sculpted into the image of Jesus, stands.

That experience still resonates in my heart—begging me to be quicker to show mercy rather than anger, to exhibit love to those who offend me, to forgive as I would want to be forgiven, and to extend charity to my enemy. What a different world this would be, amidst all of the vitriol and acrimony, if we could kill our pride and act . . . just like Jesus.

So I give you a new command: Love each other deeply and fully. Remember the ways that I have loved you, and demonstrate your love for others in those same ways. Everyone will know you as My followers if you demonstrate your love to others.

JOHN 13:34–35

Failure to recognize the value of mere being with God, as the beloved, without doing anything, is to gouge the heart out of Christianity.

EDWARD SCHILLEBEECKX

CHAPTER 9

THE REAL DEAL
OF HUMILITY

Love one another, forgive one another, work as unto God,
let the peace of Christ reign in your hearts.
Make it your ambition to lead quiet lives. Obey.
Greet another with a holy kiss. No one will argue with that.
RICH MULLINS

We all experience heartache. Often elicited by circumstances beyond our control, the pangs of brokenness only affirm that which our souls suspect—we are not yet whole.

Prompted by pain, we feel the tension between this segment of life and life forever, and we waver dangling between the finite limitations of our minds and bodies and the eternal realities of our hearts and souls. In this constant push and pull, we doubt, and doubt develops questions, and questions often create confusion, and with confusion comes humility. True humility. And humility—though costly—births hope.

Born from distressing hardships and matured through the courage to meet (rather than avoid) life's inexplicable mysteries, humility inspires us to seek a direction rather than a diagnosis. It is weighted with surrender. Though our human nature is resistant, our soulful nature is pining to just *let go*. Within the posture of surrender our hearts relax towards God, and when our hearts are open to God, we begin to really live.

Humility's gift is compassion. People attuned to the conundrum of life swell with empathy—the benefit of their conflict is the kindness of understanding and the space to partner with those who have lost, and lost a lot. Their contribution is presence, the sweet opportunity to shoulder up with and encourage those stricken by grief, while understanding they cannot, nor is it their responsibility to, extract the pain.

Most of us did not know Rich personally, but many of us knew his music. Through the compassionate content of his songs, we felt Rich identified with how much life hurts. Though his music did not provide answers to our questions, it did give us permission to ask them. More than songs to sing, Rich gave us prayers to pray.

Those who have most effectively ministered to me in

my most dire time of need have been those who, like Rich, recognize their own woundedness. They forego offering immediate counsel, reciting a Scripture or cliché condolences, and instead wordlessly say, "I don't get this either. But I'm here." Rich seemed to surround himself with these same type of people. People who just get it. They are the ones I choose again and again to live with in the most intimate manner. They are God's grace and salvation in my life, minute by minute, day by day. It is they who will usher me into eternity, and I can imagine Jesus saying to them, "Thank you for not letting him go. I love him."

Embrace the real deal of humility. Smile, greet, and search for those who will help deliver you safely to Jesus. Through being pressed down by humility's refining force, we are resurrected and transformed—healthier, more effective, and, ultimately, whole. Through humility, we find our way home.

We also celebrate in seasons of suffering because we know that when we suffer we develop endurance, which shapes our characters. When our characters are refined, we learn what it means to hope and anticipate God's goodness.

ROMANS 5:3–4

His attention and affection was not won by the attractive and the beautiful—His glance and His love made things and people attractive and beautiful.

RICH MULLINS

CHAPTER 10

LISTEN AND LOVE

David Mullins

*Our faith becomes real when we focus on what
never changes instead of our ever-changing opinions.*

RICH MULLINS

A vital message for our world today is a message of love. It is the same message Jesus scandalized the first-century people with by eating with tax collectors and sinners. He proclaimed the forgiveness of sins for the woman known for her sinful life who washed His feet with her tears and dried them with her hair, and for the man crippled since birth, not just the Jewish Pharisees who looked like they had already received it. To the religious that was distasteful in theory and repulsive in action.

As we divide ourselves over things that will not last

(and therefore are powerless to bring lasting hope), the message of Christ gets lost. As believers in this Messiah who loved and received all who would come to Him, it is our role to love and receive all who would come to Him as well. These are the reasons Jesus's message of love needs to be lived out in our modern world.

One of the most important ways to create an open environment is to listen. In a culture in which everyone is shouting, we can love through genuinely listening to the people we encounter—not listening to find a flaw in their logic or argument, but listening to hear what they desire and what they long for in their core. Rich asked questions, then listened. As a result, he really heard people. And loved them.

What do others value? What are they afraid of? If we could talk less and listen more, we might more closely identify with others. Wasn't that the reason Jesus came to the earth? He wore our flesh in order to identify with us. He was tempted and tried as we are tempted and tried. When we follow His example in identifying with the lives of others, we may care about people in a way that reveals the love of Christ—in a way that opens the door for Him to draw them to Himself.

Examine your conversations. How much time do you spend listening to someone to understand them, rather than speaking or thinking about what you will say next?

See if listening does not begin to build a culture where people feel welcomed even when you disagree.

Jesus related with those He met as people first. Then He was able to share with them the love that redeems us and can reestablish our original design to bear the image of God. It's that simple: listen and love.

My loved ones, let us devote ourselves to loving one another. Love comes straight from God, and everyone who loves is born of God and truly knows God. Anyone who does not love does not know God, because God is love.

1 JOHN 4:7–8

O most grateful burden, which comforts them that carry it! The burdens of earthly masters gradually wear out the strength of those who carry them; but the burden of Christ assists the bearers of it, because we carry not grace, but grace us.

SAINT JOHN CHRYSOSTOM

CHAPTER 11

GRIEF'S PATIENT FRIEND

*The dominant characteristic of an authentic spiritual life
is the gratitude that flows from trust—not only
for all the gifts that I receive from God, but gratitude for all
the suffering. Because in that purifying experience, suffering
has often been the shortest path to intimacy with God.*

BRENNAN MANNING

Rich was so very relatable, in part because he was open about the pain in his own life. He was not only aware of it, he was honest about it. And if we are being honest, as long as there is breath in our lungs, we will be confronted with pain sometime in our life. Though it is easy to pin its persistence on "original sin"—when that pernicious enemy tempted humankind with a lust for knowledge—pain remains a complicated matter.

Most of us have had a poignant personal association with suffering. I have been taught, and have come
to believe, that life is a gift from God, but if life is one of
His good endowments to us, why does it cause us so much
hurt? The sting of grief elicits a long list of inquiries beginning and ending with "Why, God?" And understandably
so. Surely if God knew how bad life hurt, He would eliminate heartache on the spot.

I, too, have petitioned the heavens with a chorus of
"why." I have yet to receive a clear reply from God, or
the heavens, or even a self-help book—at least any sort
of response of which I can make sense. So in fear of my
questions becoming merely rhetorical, I reopened the
Scriptures and thumbed through the pages in hopes of
discovering some golden ticket of enlightenment.

I re-noticed how often Jesus's ministry was clobbered
by crowds of people with requests and questions. He was
consistently surrounded by others—He was rarely alone—
but it seems He was also seldom really known. The burden of bringing eternal purpose to earth must have left
Him feeling isolated and alone. And Jesus, like any other
human being, needed the confidence and the comfort of
a few close companions. The disciples were Jesus's "professional" nucleus, His cohorts, involved and essential to
kingdom business. But Mary, Martha, and Lazarus were
Jesus's people. They were His posse, cronies, comrades,

buds—His coveted inner circle. They loved Jesus, not just because He was their deliverer, but because He was their friend. They knew each other well, and they liked each other a lot.

When Jesus hears of Lazarus's death, He first accepts the spiritual assignment—to bring Lazarus back from the dead. Resurrection is in Jesus's wheelhouse, and demonstrating God's power as an example of His compassion and concern for human life has been a central focus of Jesus's life on earth from the beginning. But as He arrives in Bethany, the place where Lazarus has been buried, Jesus is attuned to the grief of His friends, and for a moment He ceases to operate as the commissioned Messiah and is compelled to connect with His friends through the very human emotion of sadness. And in the middle of God's glorious redemption revelation, two tender words, one poignant action, stops us dead in our tracks . . . "Jesus *wept*."

Let that short sentence linger in your mind until the truth that it uncovers becomes palpable in your heart. Arguably, more than any other parable, declaration, or philosophy presented in the Gospels, the tenderness of Jesus's emotion identifies us *completely* with Him. God cried.

And with just the turn of a phrase, we are assured that God is not avoiding our pain. He is not out of touch. He is not absent. He is not just the Most High, but He is the

Down Close. With the shedding of tears we are assured that He is not simply our larger-than-life Creator, but He is our closest friend.

I suppose God could snap His fingers, wave a wand, wrinkle His nose, and eradicate pain from here to kingdom come in an instant. But in thinking about it, more than some arbitrary answer or comprehensive dogma, what I'm looking for is a friend. And there, in the throes of grief, I found Him.

Out of emptiness he came, like a tender shoot from rock-hard ground. He didn't look like anything or anyone of consequence—He had no physical beauty to attract our attention. So he was despised and forsaken by men, this man of suffering, grief's patient friend.

ISAIAH 53:2–3

CHAPTER 12

THE RESOLUTION
OF GRACE

*The object of a New Year is not that we should have
a new year. It is that we should have a new soul
and a new nose; new feet, a new backbone, new ears,
and new eyes. Unless a particular man made
New Year resolutions, he would make no resolutions.
Unless a man starts afresh about things,
he will certainly do nothing effective.*

G. K. CHESTERTON

I have never been a big fan of New Year's Eve. Prompted by the flip of the calendar, folks around the world make (and break) a list of resolutions pertaining to every facet of health and wellness marketable to man. Far and wide, throngs of otherwise civilized people crowd metropolitan city centers (is anyone else an introvert?) to roast the old and toast the new at the midnight stroke of January the first. (What about February the first?)

To top off the chaos, the earth is typically frozen— Mother Nature expressing her feelings about the whole shebang.

New Year's Eve is hardly the problem. Truth be told, I have never been fond of hype, not even when it pertains to me. Try and congratulate me, pat me on the back, hail a career achievement, or call attention to a personal milestone and my eyes dart to the floor, I stutter "Thanks," and proceed to water down the praise with phrases like "There are many others more talented." "You could have written that song, that book, that blog," and so forth.

The habit of circumventing commendations is hardly some isolated gene or trait exclusive to me. False humility plagues us all. I have been on the receiving end of a diffident rebuttal to my attempts at voicing appreciation for the gift of someone's obvious talents and accomplishments

In the chorus of compliments, why is a "thank you" so tough? Why do we find it so difficult to receive proper kudos?

Perhaps I deflect approval because I believe I am not worth the approval. Perhaps I shy away from applause because I simply do not believe I am worthy of the applause. Perhaps we find loving others troublesome because we have yet to believe we are worth being loved.

Ralph Waldo Emerson penned these words over 150 years ago: "Write it on your heart that every day is the best day in the year." Amended for the sake of spiritual personalization, Emerson's words might read: "Write it on your heart every day, nay, every second, that you belong, that you matter, and you are loved."

Believe it. It's not hogwash. It is not some frilly feel-good expression. The truth that we are loved by our Creator "as is," 100 percent, no strings attached, is the resolution of grace—a resolution that is renewed every single day and can never be broken.

Consider the kind of extravagant love the Father has lavished on us—He calls us children of God! It's true; we are His beloved *children.*

1 JOHN 3:1

Rich Mullins - Goals & Resolutions for 1998

My goal is to stop being grumpy.

My resolution is my plan of attack:

a. get up before I have to so I can have a half hour at least before I have to talk to anyone.

b. cut back on chemicals.

c. spend an hour each early evening working out — do not hurry.

d. unplug my phone — use my answering machine as a dart board. Throw ice cubes at it when I'm frustrated instead of making cutting remarks to people I love.

e. stop expecting big successes and start celebrating the little ones.

d. chart the movements of the big dipper & soak in the sun as much as possible. Live in a world that is bigger than my calendar — more permanent than my feelings, more glorious than my accomplishments. (that should be easy.)

CHAPTER 13

HOW RUDE . . .
NOT TO AGREE WITH GOD

Mark Lowry

Christ loved the sons of men before there were sons of men,
and me before there was me. If he was going to get tired
of me, he would have done so before now.

CHARLES HADDON SPURGEON

A year or two before Rich died, he and I had been invited as guest artists on Sandi Patty's Caribbean cruise. He brought Mitch McVicker, and I brought my friend Norman Holland. We ported at St. Martin's Island for a day and it was decided the four of us would rent scooters. So we jumped off the ship, piled into a cab, and asked the driver to "Take us to a scooter place!" We thought he probably had some friend out in the woods he could work with for a deal. I had my wallet, because I wanted to pay for the excursion, but nobody else brought anything.

The driver ended up taking us on this long ride and I thought, *This is my chance!* I finally had the time to talk with Rich Mullins about God and all the things I wanted to ask him—what I was thinking through theologically and spiritually at the time. We talked, time flew, and the next thing I knew we were in the middle of the woods at this shack with a few scooters. We got out, I handed over my credit card, and we scooted away, never paying attention to where we were going. We were just excited to take off!

We were having the best time scooting around the island when I realized, if we didn't head back, we were going to miss the ship. We kept circling, trying to find the scooter rental shop, and when we finally found it and returned the scooters . . . we had missed the boat. Since the ship was at sea, we spent the night on the island and had an incredible time.

I was thinking about so much at that time, questioning, *Does God really like me? Do I really believe the right thing? Is Christianity really true? Are we just on a rabbit trail? Are we just believing this because we have been taught this all of our lives? If I had been born in Syria, would I have been Islamic?* Having the opportunity to discuss these questions with Rich was awesome.

I had basically come to the decision that Christianity worked for me. I chose to believe it whether I felt it or not. I was a Christian agnostic—I believed a lot, I knew nothing. But belief is enough. If you don't have some big Damascus road experience where life knocks you off your donkey and you are blind for three days, choosing to believe is important.[8] Think about Paul. God really had to work with him, to get him to believe, but we are more blessed than Paul because Jesus said, "Blessed are those who have not seen and yet have believed."[9] I have seen nothing, so according to Jesus, I am the more blessed because I believe.

I have chosen to go down this path with Christ; whatever He says, I believe it. The pot does not get to tell the potter what the pot's worth. The potter tells the pot what the pot's worth; the pot doesn't get a vote. Who am I to tell the Creator, "You messed up when you made me"? I am exactly who He wants me to be. Even the things I have done I pray the world never finds out about, they are a part of the journey, a part of the patchwork on the quilt of who I am. I'm pretty disgusting, but God likes me. He's working with me. He is not impatient. He's long-suffering, and I have never felt condemned in God's presence. I have felt convicted. I have felt condemned in the presence of His people, but never in His presence. If you feel condemned in the presence of Jesus, fire him, you have the wrong one. He didn't come to condemn us, but to deliver us. *There is now no condemnation for those who are in Christ Jesus.*[10]

How rude not to agree with God. So I agree with Him. Rich helped me learn how to do that. Rich lived as if he really believed God loved him. That was new for me. I am grateful now, but it took me a long time to get there.

The day after our accidental island layover, the four of us had to fly from St. Martin's to Miami to the Bahamas, going in and out of customs, to catch the ship, and I was the only one who had a wallet—in other words, the only one with money and a driver's license—so I talked us through each checkpoint. When we finally hooked up with the cruise, we realized our friends didn't know if we were dead or alive. Rich and I crawled across the stage, on our hands and knees, begging Sandi to forgive us for messing up the program. She obliged.

When Rich passed away, I called Sandi and said, "I can't tell you how thankful I am that I missed the ship."

But for all who did receive and trust in Him, He gave them the right to be reborn as children of God; He bestowed this birthright not by human power or initiative but by God's will.

JOHN 1:12–13

CHAPTER 14

HUM A HYMN

Music gives a soul to the universe, wings to the mind,
flight to the imagination, and life to everything.

PLATO

There is an art to singing. A certain mercy in telling the truth through a lyric that, when compelled by a beautiful melody, translates an idea from the mind into a life-altering reality that changes the heart. Rich's songs were especially merciful.

For whatever reason, God has infused music with Himself. The universal appeal and emotion of rhythm and rhyme is a testament to music's spiritual motivation. Songs transcend our cultural differences, political bias, religious affiliations, and language barriers to unify us through the refrain that belongs to every man—love.

In 1992 Sarajevo was riven by the duress of the Bosnian War. Vedran Smailović, the principal cellist for the Sarajevo Opera, traveled with his instrument to spots in the city where combat had killed innocent civilians. He set up shop and, with wartime shrapnel whirring around his melodious post, contributed to peace in the only way he knew how—by playing music. As residents heard the heartache of his bow press into the strings, they came out from their hidings and for a moment surrendered the bleak outlook of their current circumstances to embrace hope through the sound of music.

> To sing to God amidst sorrow is to defiantly proclaim . . . that death is not the final word. To defiantly say, once again, that a light shines in the darkness and the darkness cannot, will not, shall not overcome it. And so, evil be damned, because even as we go to the grave, we still make our song alleluia. Alleluia. Alleluia.
>
> NADIA BOLZ-WEBER

In the midst of the conflicts of our lives—the shame cycled from low self-esteem, the scarlet letter branded from one poor decision long ago, the what-ifs that plague the conscience of the one left behind—music tunes up a lifeline of hope and sings out a conversation with God.

I grew up with church hymns. Some kids prize a special storybook, a favorite tree, or a sports team, but I treasured an old Baptist hymnal. The hymns are where I first encountered God.

Messages of unconditional love and grace and friendship with the Creator permeated the vintage verses of that glorious songbook. If ever I doubted my worth, I could open up that time-tested hymnal and lessons of love would flood my mind, ears, and heart. As I sang those songs that have pursed the lips and shaped the faith of generations of truth-seekers, the understanding that "God loves" in my mind transforms into a deep, generous belief in my heart that God loves *me* in my heart.

Live long enough and the experience of life will fluctuate between high highs and low lows. We will live days of profound joy and moments of deep sadness. We will get beat up a little, some of us a lot, and we just won't know if we are hitting the mark—in life, in relationships, in commitments with our communities, and in interactions with friends. Thankfully, there is a great grace in music. For when we surrender the song that the spirit is nurturing within our souls through the exercise of singing, our spiritual demeanor transforms from simply reciting deep eternal truths to embodying the reality of them in our everyday lives—a liturgy to legacy, of sorts.

So in the very middle of our many pains and losses, when seeking a dose of comfort and a lot of perspective, try humming a hymn.

Sing the psalms, compose hymns and songs inspired by the Spirit, and keep on singing—sing to God from hearts full and spilling over with thankfulness.

COLOSSIANS 3:16

CHAPTER 15

A Little Salt in the Oats

Jason Gray

*I have failed enough that I've learned
that it's not the end of the world to make mistakes.*
RICH MULLINS

"I traveled by myself for several years and had a lot of struggles . . . 'cause it's just so hard to not watch those movies in your hotel room when you're alone," he says with a smile that is so many things at once—sad, funny, vulnerable, disarming. Though the road has taken a toll, you can still see that boyish spark behind his eyes that somehow looks like he's ready to pick a fight with you and make you his best friend at the same time.

Rich Mullins is introducing "Hold Me Jesus," one of his most tender anthems about the love of God, as he shares from stage a story that implies that, even as one of Christian music's most beloved artists, he has struggled with pornography—ministering God's love by day and stumbling into private sin by night.

It is a holy moment and I am grateful someone had the wherewithal to capture it on film and post it online years later for people like me. The clip is titled "Beaker Wouldn't Snore," and I'm watching it, as I have watched it more times than I can count over the years.

Rich's stage story is not a very shocking confession as far as confessions go (and mild compared to other Rich Mullins's stories I have heard), but I suppose it feels potent because it's hard for me to imagine such a prominent artist in today's Christian music industry—including myself—being as forthright and transparent.

In Rich's apparent disregard for his own reputation, we get the sense that he is not trying to protect anything. He isn't wearing any armor. There is a reckless generosity in the way Rich throws himself under the bus so that we can catch a glimpse of what the unfailing love of God looks like in the honest-to-God life of a broken, beloved, sinful child of God. Rich's transparency about his messiness helps me believe that I might be loved in my mess, too.

Have we regressed since Rich was alive? Even when these kinds of struggles are spoken of from a public platform, today, they are more likely to be dressed up in "victorious believer" language, skipping over entire chapters of the redemptive story in a mad dash to some happy ending. *I struggled with this once, but because of Jesus I don't anymore and you don't have to either.* This is a different flavor of admission than I taste in Rich's confession. In Rich's story I taste the salt.

A mentor of mine told me, "Though you can lead a horse to water, you can't make him drink. But you can make him thirsty by mixing a little salt in the oats." Rich's oats were salty. His disregard for his own reputation makes me thirsty for more of the living water his music has led me to again and again. His transparency makes me long to trust God more and put less hope in pleasing people, in propping up a pretty version of myself so they will give me the support, career, and admiration I long for. Rich's honesty makes me want to risk showing off the unfailing love that heals honest-to-God broken, beloved, sinful children of God, like me, and like Rich, even if that means surrendering my own reputation.

After several more salty revelations, Rich sings, "*Hold me, Jesus 'cause I'm shaking like a leaf.*" In that ragged voice I hear the hope that calls me to trust that I am held, and for a moment I feel so securely embraced that I might even dare risk being transparent enough for people to see beyond me—just one more broken, beloved, sinful child of God—so they might catch a vision of the King of my glory, the Prince of my peace . . . the One whose love never fails.

Thankfully, God does not punish us for our sins and depravity as we deserve.

In His mercy, He tempers justice with peace.

Measure how high heaven is above the earth;

God's wide, loving, kind heart is greater for those who revere Him.

You see, God takes all our crimes—our seemingly inexhaustible sins—and removes them.

As far as east is from the west, He removes them from us.

PSALM 103:10–12

CHAPTER 16

A CONVERSATION WITH ANDREW PETERSON

Andrew Peterson is often touted as a modern-day Rich Mullins. Though this is a comparison he has been cautious to receive because of his great respect for Rich and the deep influence he had on Andrew's music and life, a study of their songwriting reveals the likeness.

Q: What did you witness in Rich's life and lyrics that you try to embody in your own life and lyrics?

Andrew Peterson: Rich made me want to believe the gospel more than I did. I was a nineteen-year-old kid in a rock band, and I was really frightened of God. I didn't like myself at all, and to be honest, a lot of days I still don't. I was just lost, wandering around in the world trying to figure out what I was supposed to do. I believed that there was some great beauty out there, but I could never articulate what it was or why I was looking for it.

The first time I heard him in concert was at my little Bible college in Florida. When he talked about God, I got the sense that he was talking about an actual person that he actually *knew*, not about an idea. I wanted that. I was *so* hungry for that. I'm hungry for it now.

A person recently told my pastor, "I have a hard time feeling close to God." My pastor replied, "When was the last time you did something for someone else?" I remember Rich saying if you want to know God, or be close to God, obey Him. Go do the things that He's called us to do. Rich wasn't perfect, but I think he tried to live his life as if the gospel were true. That way of living resonated with a lot of people who, like me, were hungry for the gospel and wanted it so badly.

Rich's music was this combination of Scripture and poetry and humanity. His songs were full of Scripture, and they could be loftily poetic, but they were also very human, using folky vernacular. He brought all these big, beautiful ideas down to earth, and he sang about them with an earthy voice. In a key that I could actually sing in. To feel like you've been given a gift of some kind but you have no paradigm for expressing it was very frustrating. So for a young guy who wasn't a good singer, but felt like he had a song to sing, hearing Rich's music gave me permission to try—I didn't have to be perfect or slick if I wanted to write songs.

Q: In our churches, it seems there is a gap between connecting with God as our father and discovering Him as our friend—as this personal God. Do you feel like putting "skin" on God has been a part of your own musical trajectory and why you continue to write songs?

Andrew: George MacDonald wrote, "A poet is someone who is glad about something and wants other people to be glad about it, too." Sometimes a songwriter is someone who feels captured by the wonder of something and wants somebody else to be captured by it, too. *Come, I want to show you something that I saw.* An encounter with Jesus is the deepest version of that. *I had an encounter with love, and with beauty, and truth, and that person has a name and I want you to know that name, too.*

I was the recipient of that through Rich and his music. I was in Bible college when I heard "The Love of God," and when the chorus ends with, *"In the reckless raging fury that they call the love of God,"* I just wept because I couldn't believe it. "Is that really who He is?" "Does He really love me that way?" So as a songwriter, one of my highest callings would be to make Jesus known, and one of the ways I do that is by telling my story about who He is in my life.

It wasn't until I heard Rich talk about God as a person that I believed that it could be true. I'm so frightened of being known. One of the main things that keeps coming up in my life and music is this fear that once people really know me they won't like me anymore. Or worse, they might despise me. I project that fear on to God, and onto Jesus, so my tendency to hide from Him is a habit that I'm constantly trying to push back. Going to church is a way for me to fight that habit—to go to a place where I'm known, and can go to the table every Sunday and be assured that the One who knows me best loves me most.

Q: Within Rich's songwriting there is a constant longing for home, for something we haven't yet experienced. I sense that throughout your music as well.

Andrew: The church is living in that tension. We believe something has happened, but something is still going to happen, and that keeps us alive in some way. The longing reminds us the story's not over.

The end of the Nicene Creed reads, "We look for the resurrection and the life of the world to come." I often get emotional when we get to that part because the church has said all of these things that we believe, so now what? What do we do with all that? Well, we look for the resurrection and the life of the world to come. We're constantly leaning into that.

In *Surprised by Joy*, C. S. Lewis talks about *sehnsucht*—the German word for an "inconsolable longing"—and how the breadcrumbs that led him to faith in Christ were these moments of *sehnsucht*, these stabs of almost painful joy that he couldn't explain. God peppers all of our lives with these moments, and part of our job as members of the human race is to follow the breadcrumbs and ask, "Okay, why did *that* get my attention?" "Why was I crying during *that* movie?" "What was it about that story that got me?" Buechner talks about listening to your life. Pay attention to your life and you'll discover, hopefully, what it is that God is wanting you to ultimately see—grace.

If I were to look back on the works of art that got my attention—that category of art and literature that did something transcendent in my life—they would be *Lord of the Rings*, Buechner's books, Wendell Berry's *Jayber Crow*, the Narnia books, and it would be Rich Mullins's music. It got my attention in a way that nothing else ever has, and it still makes me cry. I'll spend my whole life trying to understand why.

Q: We live in a divided culture. We are so strained by social issues, by politics and platforms—we exist separately rather than together. Love is often trumpeted as what will bring us together, but is the solution to such deep divides really as simple as love?

Andrew: It's not a question of *our* love, but God's love for us. Brennan Manning said, "I am now utterly convinced that on Judgment Day Jesus is going to ask each of us one question, and only one question, 'Did you believe that I loved you?'"[11]

If I'm honest with myself, most of every day I don't believe that Jesus loves me. Even though He has provided mountains of evidence to the contrary, I'm so convinced that I'm a screwup that no matter how much I try to work that out by doing nice things, the effort is all flesh, not spirit. These actions pale in comparison to those moments of transcendence, of real grace, where I'm stopped in my tracks by something beautiful that actually breaks through the noise in my head and the narrative that I've told myself for my whole life—it shatters that just for a second, and the voice of God breaks through and says, "You're loved." And even if just for a moment, I have the grace to believe it. That's why I'm so bonkers about reading books and watching movies and listening to music—I'm always on the hunt for evidence that there is a God and that He really does love me.

Maybe it's a better thing to be more than merely innocent, but to be broken and then redeemed by love. This is what the forces of darkness don't understand about what God is up to: He's in the process of not merely making us innocent, like babes, but He's in the process of redeeming who we are now, and making us into these resurrected creatures whose stories we bear just like Christ bore the scars of the cross. And the scars of the cross make Him more, not less, glorious. This is what our sadness, what all of this grief we're experiencing, is reflecting. In the end, I have to believe that Christ is the model for what it is that God is doing for us, and that these wounds are making us more beautiful.

Top: Rich's reaction to unexpectedly seeing his concert poster during a walk through a small town in Ohio.
Bottom: Visiting the church with David McCracken, where Rich served as youth minister in Kentwood, Michigan.

PART 2

THUNDER

Relationship Versus Religion

Christianity is not about building an absolutely secure little niche in the world where you can live with your perfect little wife, and your perfect little children, in your beautiful little house, where you have no gays or minority groups anywhere near you. Christianity is about learning to love like Jesus loved, and Jesus loved the poor and Jesus loved the broken.

RICH MULLINS[1]

On stage with Steve Cudworth, Rich's co-writer and sideman (1986–1988). Together they wrote the CCM classic, "If I Stand."

THUNDER

You walked in when the prophets had grown tired
Of being so inspired but rarely being heard
Coming on to a world confused and scattered
The silence was shattered by the power of the Word.

It sounded like thunder when You cleared the temple
Sounded like thunder sometimes when You prayed
Incredible wonder when the veil was torn in glory
Sounded like thunder when the stone was rolled away.

You spoke truth, You sat among the people
They listened in amazement at all the things You said
Like a storm that rose above the quiet
The sound of Your love was enough to raise the dead.

When I think about You giving and loving and crying
And suffering our pain
When I think about You living and dying and rising
My tears fall like rain.

RICH MULLINS, PHIL NAISH, AND LOWELL ALEXANDER[2]

Playing the hammered dulcimer in concert.

Part 2

INTRODUCTION

In a letter to his brother, Theo, post-impressionist nineteenth-century painter Vincent van Gogh wrote, "I am no friend of present-day Christianity, though its Founder was sublime."[3]

The jab at the religion was drafted because of a frustration with his family's displeasure over Vincent's fatal attraction to maniacal women, probably for "Christian" reasons. But the famous artist's disgruntlement with his family's Christian concern is relevant in our twenty-first-century church culture, where orthodoxy is often used as a two-edged tool for propagating a variety of human-led agendas rather than constructing a Jesus-led kingdom.

Christianity's mark on culture throughout the last two millennia has little to do with the laws its religion has protected, but rather the life of Jesus it pronounces. Jesus's life, death, and resurrection continue to thunder throughout the climate of our culture, and our hearts, today.

In his own letters to local first-century churches throughout the Middle East and Eastern Europe, the apostle Paul warned Christian believers of pharisaical members—"busybodies"[4] more concerned with a self-serving, self-righteous doctrine of appearances than the gospel of Jesus that motivates us to serve others and gifts us with the righteousness of God living in and through us.

And throughout His life here on earth, Jesus always chose relationship with people over religion. When the dead-end letter of the law threatened to outcast His living letter of love, elevating pious practices of church tradition over a practical hands-and-feet ministry to the common man, Jesus religiously protested. His own brother, James, transcribed the aim of Christian discipleship, writing, "Real, true religion from God the Father's perspective is about caring for orphans and widows who suffer needlessly and resisting the evil influence of the world."[5]

Rich chafed against the paint-by-numbers parameters of the gospel music industry. From his ragamuffin perspective, his choice was clear: he could either appease the mass-market demands of a religiously "right" constituency by softening his creed and diluting his dialogue, or he could appeal to people's hearts through honest and human exchanges.

It wasn't that Rich didn't love spiritual traditions. In fact, according to the recollections of those who lived alongside him, Rich had an insatiable appetite for Scripture. He had a thorough knowledge of the Bible. And he was neither unaware nor unaffected by the ancient tenets of Christian beliefs. But he had no tolerance for religion without result. Instead, he pored over Scripture's holy revelations for the inspiration to love and serve others better by loving and serving God more deeply.

And it seems, when you examine the relationships his music brought him and the conversation his life instigated, for Rich, it worked.

Whether through his unconcerned, barefooted stage "dress," his itinerant living habits, or his extraordinary devotion to his band mates, Rich's relationships were an offspring of his apparent uninhibited abandon to the intent of the gospel. Even today, through his life and lyrics, Rich's persuasive faith thunders through the hallowed spaces of our spiritual discourse—prompting us to think, to change, and to surrender—to truly and utterly, as Rich often wrote, "be God's."

Rich and Cindy Morgan sing "Have Yourself a Merry Little Christmas" at the 1994 *Release* Magazine Christmas Party, Nashville, Tennessee.

CHAPTER 17

JUXTAPOSITION

Dan Haseltine from Jars of Clay

By loving we participate in His life and essence.
RICH MULLINS

Even though the human form—something as intoxicating as skin and movement—is beautiful, the human instinct that lurks underneath our flesh is terrifying. Left to our own devices, with only our most primal instincts leading us, we become harbingers of destructive behavior. Unchecked, this instinct curates genocides and torture, tyranny, starvation, and war. Humanity is a threat unto itself. To serve our motives and ambitions, we will fight—even to death.

But then there's grace, the thing God has gifted upon and within humanity. Grace allows us to believe humanity can be light and life. When the light of grace drives out darkness, it does not also drive out humanity. Rather, even in humanity's depravity, grace collaborates with us to create something fertile and excessively loving.

I first met Rich Mullins after a Jars of Clay show. Cigarette hanging from his lip, face reflecting the glow from a small flame dancing above his cheap truck stop lighter, he said to me, "If you're gonna show your [rear end] to people, it better be to a bunch of Christians."

At that point in my religious experience Christians were angry, fearful creatures. They were flag-planters who fashioned agreements about how God worked, but when those agreements were scrutinized, or when their moral doctrines became obsolete, the Christians I knew stood ready and steady to aim and fire.

I wanted to tell Rich that Christians are the wrong sort to show your vices and failures to, but I think he loved the juxtaposition.

One year later, on a suffocatingly humid Nashville day in late August, my wife and I were married. My pastor, an emotional, charismatic man brimming with compassion and love, based our wedding sermon on a woman on the verge of being stoned by a community who knew her only as a whore. Rescued by Jesus, by most retellings, He then commands her to "Go and sin no more."

It was an unusual story for celebrating matrimony, but

as the dramatic story unfolds, the beautiful slow dance of humanity and grace begins to form.

When the woman's accusers ambush her at the well, they too are guilty. No one in the scene is clean. No matter who was potentially "righteous" or "good," the crowd was poised to stone a person to death. They were primed for murder. And no matter how much I wanted the woman to be innocent, the story is clear, she was a prostitute, and it does not appear she was forced into the profession by some poverty-stricken circumstance or dramatic need. More than likely, her liaisons had destroyed some local families.

As Jesus interrupts and relieves the tension, I, like most, interpreted His directive to sin no more as a command rather than an act of compassion. *Why would Jesus save her only to turn around and judge her?* I didn't understand His tone. The narrative lost me, and so I set it down.

The story felt like it was lying to me.

But what my pastor knew, and what I have since learned—and in line with how Rich lived—the end of the story matters.

As Jesus spoke to the scarleted seducer, the Scripture's author notes that Jesus knew the woman. In that moment I imagine Him whispering to her, "Do you see? You are believing things about yourself that are not true. You sin because you are afraid. But do you see what I see in you?"

As He spoke to her, suddenly she felt known. Not as

a one-dimensional façade, or the sum of her failures, but as the universe she truly was. And in being known completely by God, she received the gift of seeing herself as He sees her. And so He says, "Go. You don't have to sin anymore. You are whole. You are beloved. You are known."

Who then should be able to respond with grace to the many vices and failures of humanity? Christians. Not as some self-righteous stewards of judgment, but as people known by God, and so whose humanity has been married with grace.

Jesus: Dear woman, where is everyone? Are we alone? Did no one step forward to condemn you?

Woman Caught in Adultery: Lord, no one has condemned me.

Jesus: Well, I do not condemn you either; all I ask is that you go and from now on avoid the sins that plague you.

JOHN 8:10–11

CHAPTER 18

THE POWER OF PRESENCE

We want to go to God for answers,
but sometimes what we get is God's presence.

Nadia Bolz-Weber

From the time we gasp in our first breath of air until the day we breathe out our last, we are captured by life and the range of circumstances and emotions it embodies. Rich's poetic songwriter perspective captured those raw emotions and spun them into something beautiful.

I wondered recently what kind of song Rich might spin for a friend of mine in the throes of acute pain. His losses have been great. When the shock that protected his sanity wore off, he fully felt the depth of his loss. Sad, afraid, and lonely, he was exhausted. I knew he was tempted to drown in the sorrows of his tragedy, so I drove over to his house and prodded him into the outside world.

As we sat in his car, he voiced his fears and described the loss that had left him stunned. I didn't say a word. I just listened. I could not remedy his situation, but I could be present, and somehow in the safe space of our friendship he knew that though I did not understand the intimate details of his pain, I could relate to how badly he hurt.

In Scripture, Isaiah describes Jesus as "grief's patient friend."[6] Perhaps this is what he meant—that the Messiah's presence isn't an immediate solution for the problem. He doesn't prevent the tragedy. Instead, He walks alongside us, shoulder to shoulder, with all the thoughts and feelings and questions we have, identifying with how we hurt.

Life is full of pain. We have maneuvered around it. Avoided it at all costs. Spent hard-earned cash on counseling to move through and over it. As long as there is this breath in our lungs, no matter our socioeconomic status or family background or religious inclination, we will all encounter pain. Yet the ache of the heart is not simply some great injustice or negative unfairness. Just as physical pain sends up a faithful flare to notify our minds that something in our body has gone awry, giving us an opportunity to seek aid, emotional pain triggers our feelings and raises our awareness of a surfacing wound or trauma that, once surrendered to the light with confession, can now be tended to and healed.

With a little bit of hope and a whole lot of time, the

wounds of life become scars that cultivate compassion and help us identify with others, and ultimately compel us towards God. Perhaps the point of eternity is not our healing but His nearness—not our peace but His presence.

When someone is hurting or brokenhearted, the Eternal moves in close and revives him in his pain.

PSALM 34:18

There are these skies—skies stretched so tight you just know you're about to pop standing beneath them. Your lungs may burst from breathing their sizable air—air from the cool heights so tall they scrape the footings of heaven—skies so pure and strong that God built His New Jerusalem on their back. And they reach up toward that Holy City like Romeo scaling the forbidden wall beneath Juliet—skies that go endlessly, nearly forever with the beauty of her face, the quiet, unshaken gaze of her eyes, skies alive with all the virility and tenderness of young love—skies as ancient as time, as innocent as babies held in the Hands of Eternity.

RICH MULLINS[7]

CHAPTER 19

REFLECTIONS ON RICH

Josh Blakesley

We walk by faith and not by sight because there are places
to go that cannot be seen and the scope of our vision
is too small for our strides. Faith is not a denial of facts—
it is a broadening of focus. It does not deny the hardness
of guitar strings, it plucks them into a sweetness of sound.

RICH MULLINS

I was eighteen years old. Rich Mullins, Ashley Cleveland, and Carolyn Arends were performing on the Brother's Keeper tour at the Heymann Performing Arts Center in Lafayette, Louisiana, and I was working for a small Christian music video station called The Master Channel.

I was scheduled to interview Rich about life, the new album, the tour, and anything else that came into my enamored and ecstatic teenage brain. Only in recent years had I stepped out from behind a drum set to begin my own journey of writing and singing, so I was overflowing with questions that I *needed* to ask Rich.

He came into the room as expected: white T-shirt, blue jeans, and, of course, barefoot—exactly how he would saunter onto the stage a half-hour later.

I asked questions that I'm sure he had answered a thousand times before. *How did you get started in music? How do you spend your time when you're not on the road?* But the conversation quickly turned towards the spiritual. I still remember the butterflies in my stomach as I worked up the courage to present the one question I had been dying to ask.

Born and raised Catholic, my faith, the traditions associated with it, the close friendships I had made growing up in Catholic school, the spiritual direction I had received as a young man discerning my calling—it all escalated in my mind so profoundly in that moment. I was a young Catholic trying to break into what seemed like an industry of Protestant singers and songwriters, and here I was staring into the face of the one who had consistently challenged all the stereotypes.

The moment was especially weighted because I had heard that Rich was taking Rite of Christian Initiation (RCIA) classes. Was it true? A man who had been so involved in the Christian music world for so long was becoming a Catholic? What would this mean for Christian music? Forget Christian music, what would this mean for Christianity in the United States?

We use words like "acceptance," "integration," "unity," "solidarity," but so often only behind closed doors in rooms carpeted with eggshells. However, here was a man who had a reputation for barreling through closed doors with bare feet. He had guts and a huge platform.

So, if it were true, if Rich Mullins was joining the Catholic church, would it be a complete bombshell of division, or would it just fall silently into a deep, loving well of Christian unification? With sweaty palms, a shaky voice, and all the daring I could muster, I asked, "Rich, I hear you like to challenge yourself and your beliefs with regard to different Christian faiths. Where are you in that spiritual walk right now?"

I'm still not sure what made me more nervous: would the question offend him or would his answer offend me? Unfazed, he looked at me and said, "All I know is that I don't have all the answers. So, I'm trying to learn as much as I can about God from the people on earth who seem to know more than me."

Over twenty years ago, fifteen minutes with Rich and I learned a lesson that will stay with me for a lifetime. It's a lesson for all humanity, and it crosses religions, races, ages, and genders. Sometimes confidence in what we think we know prohibits our ability to truly understand Truth, to understand love, to understand each other. Unity—real Christian unity—comes from the ability to lower our defenses, accept realities other than our own, and be the first to say, in humility, "I don't know everything."

Lord, give me the ability to know when I just don't know and the courage to admit it. Amen.

Embrace true humility, and lift your heads to extend love to others. Get beyond yourselves and protecting your own interests; be sincere, and secure your neighbors' interests first.

PHILIPPIANS 2:3–5

CHAPTER 20

THE TRUTH OF A SUNSET

I believe in Christianity as I believe
that the sun has risen: not only because I see it,
but because by it I see everything else.

C. S. LEWIS

I once heard a story about Rich purchasing a tepee. He erected it on a piece of land in Kansas belonging to a friend. During the height of his musical career he would spend his days off living in this wigwam, no doubt deriving inspiration from the peace of the sprawling Midwestern plains. Perhaps this minimalist's retreat was a simple effort to seek solitude among nature in the middle of a noisy life of concerts and crowds. But I also like to think that Rich's affinity for living on the land was because God was so obviously evident inside the out-of-doors.

Growing up on the hem of Western America, believing in a divine Creator was fairly easy. From dusk until dawn, some divine artistry imbued the landscape with color-filled atmospheric effects, cunning creatures, and spindly shapes and shadows.

But it was the breathtaking Western sunset that captured the wide-eyed wonder of visitors and locals alike. As the parched plains rose up, and the spotless sky stooped low, the union of sky and land produced an almost eternal horizon, alluding to a forever the mind cannot yet comprehend but the soul is already beginning to grasp. The sun, a flaming ball of life-giving power, would tuck itself beneath the skyline, descending in real time from the heavens to the earth in peaceful grandeur and tired rest.

Then came the night. A billion stars, at minimum, materialized in the pitch-black sky, devising a magnificent nightlight under which the country children count sheep, and the coyotes convene.

Oh, sure, nostalgia edits out the worse parts of the plains' climate: terrible tornadoes, life-threatening ice storms, and heatstroke-inducing triple-digit temperatures. Our perspectives change as we mature and adult experience opens our eyes to ache and pain and sorrow. But some things do not change with pain. They merely deepen.

I have revisited the place of my childhood many times as an adult. Since I left, I have experienced the whips and whims of life, and at times have come out a bit worse for the wear. But the awe those wide open space induced in my heart as a child keeps burrowing deeper into a soulful core I barely remember exists until I embrace the everyday opportunity to be still, to be quiet, and with my full faculties to truly *be*.

The stories that populate the pages of Scripture paint landscapes as vivid and enticing as the Western twilight. Full of colorful characters, stubborn sinners, and scraggly saints on the prowl for the life-giving fire of a Creator's blazing heart, a debate prevails as to whether the Bible is fact or fiction, whether it tells the truth or tall tales.

I have often wondered myself if God is truly the awe-inspiring Father I discovered among Scripture's beautiful adventures with childhood wonderment, or a fundamental event unrelated to adult life.

I wonder.

But then I revisit the prophets. And the Gospels. And the apostles' letters. And even with the tenure of ache and pain and sorrow that accompanies life this side of adolescence, my faith grows wider. And my belief even deeper. And my love for God, for others, and for myself becomes even broader than I ever thought possible.

No matter how greatly we advance in academics, how we grow scientifically or how enlightened we become, it is impossible to fully uncover the evidence of what is so concretely revealed to the soul in something as simple as a sunset.

Now, I think, *God, the exhaustive I AM, persuading Moses through a burning bush?* Why not? *The spectrum of a rainbow as a sign that God is for us, not against us?* Sure. *The Almighty Maker of heaven and earth submitting Himself to the womb of a virgin to prove He is not immune to our troubles, but right here in the middle of them?* I sure hope so.

We work so hard to descry evidence of God. Maybe all we need to engage our hearts with is the truth of a sunset.

From the beginning, creation in its magnificence enlightens us to His nature. Creation itself makes His undying power and divine identity clear, even though they are invisible.

ROMANS 1:20

CHAPTER 21

THE REALITY OF MERCY

Sara Groves

---

*Christianity is one beggar telling
another beggar where he found bread.*

D. T. NILES

Rich died one month before I finished my first independent record. I never had the privilege of meeting him, but the stories about his behind-the-scenes life intrigued and influenced me. He was not caught up in being a Christian example to Christians. Hearing stories about limits he put on his salary, and the way he went to live on a reservation—he seemed committed to not sing about anything he had not lived out at some level, and that has stayed with me.

His standard for he himself to have the authority to

walk into a church and sing was not pietistic at any level—that didn't seem to be the point. It felt as if he was always saying to us, *You are asking the wrong question!*

Anyone who resides in the realm of Christian leadership for any amount of time will wrestle with the tension between publicly pronouncing belief—or creed—and falling short of those beliefs in very real ways. It is a disquieting thing to believe something so deeply, and yet live in daily conflict with what Eugene Peterson called the "Ancient Trifecta": the flesh, the world—or culture—and the devil himself.

It always felt to me that Rich Mullins's music was born in this imperfect, pell-mell, follow-me-while-I-follow-Christ place. Rich seemed to be convinced, as I am, that the best defense against these things is vulnerability about struggle, and honesty about suffering. To move against the impulse to hide failure and pain is a movement towards showing the light of grace, and the reality of lived mercy.

From my experience with Rich's music, he also sends out a very necessary message to others that clearly says, "You are not alone!" It takes someone brave enough to go first, but once someone does go first, transparency begets transparency, mercy begets mercy, vulnerability begets vulnerability—all of the things necessary for healing.

Now that we know what we have—Jesus, this great High Priest with ready access to God—let's not let it slip through our fingers. We don't have a priest who is out of touch with our reality. He's been through weakness and testing, experienced it all—all but the sin. So let's walk right up to him and get what he is so ready to give. Take the mercy, accept the help.

HEBREWS 4:14–16 MSG

"Mercy, God, mercy!": the prayer is not an attempt to get God to do what He is unwilling otherwise to do, but a reaching out to what we know that He does do, an expressed longing to receive what God is doing in and for us in Jesus Christ. . . .

We live under the mercy. God does not treat us as alien others, lining us up so that He can evaluate our competence or our usefulness or our worth. He rules, guides, commands, loves us as children whose destinies He carries in His heart.

EUGENE PETERSON

CHAPTER 22

IF THESE PEWS
COULD SPEAK

Before we had stifled the cross into a symbol,
before we had softened grace into a sentiment,
before we had systematized the power and mystery
of God's greatest revelation of Himself into a set of dogmas,
we were the children that we must become again.

RICH MULLINS

Recently, I revisited my roots and found myself darkening the doors of that strangely hallowed place where I caught my first glimpse of God over twenty-five years ago. I became a kid again. As I found my seat in my old spot on that old pew, I realized, much had remained the same.

My mom is still at the organ. Connie, my grade school music teacher, is still at the piano. Many of the faces in the choir are familiar, the blueprints of my first understanding of what it meant to be present in a service of worship to God—where I first understood authentic praise requires more than attendance, it demands a supernatural movement from the inside out. And this communion with the spirit requires surrender, which always necessitates an honest and open mind and heart (a description characteristic of many of these congregants I communed with as a child, and a description that would behoove many of us to embrace in this intensified world today).

There is a sacred space in those hardback seats. I often thought, *If these pews could speak.* All the life I have lived—the good, the messy—since my human will first collided with the spirit of God on Row Two, Right Side. Seasons of peace; moments of despair. Ecstatic joy and deep grief. Mountains of faith and valleys of doubt.

When it came time to sing, we stood, and we stood together, not in spite of our circumstances, but in and with all of them. Together our voices resonated over the beautifully administered accompaniment to sing, and to surrender, and to pray, "*Holy, holy, holy, merciful and mighty.*"

Merciful *and* mighty. Isn't He so mysteriously both? Isn't this why, even with all of our desires to push back, to pull away, to isolate and ignore, we continue to congregate? Is this not why I take my place in the pew, week after week, year after year, to petition once again with my presence, "Please, God, be merciful *and* mighty."

I need Him to be both. I need Him.

They were calling out to each other,
"Holy, holy, holy is the LORD of Heaven's Armies!
The whole earth is filled with his glory!"

ISAIAH 6:3 NLT

Sing a new song to the Eternal;
sing in one voice to the Eternal, all the earth.
Sing to the Eternal of all the good things He's done.

PSALM 96:1–2

CHAPTER 23

The Wideness in God's Mercy

Melissa Reagan

*Faith is a matter of the will
as much as it is of the intellect.*

RICH MULLINS

The lyrics of Rich Mullins are raw and honest and relatable, and we are in desperate need of hearing the truths they contain.

In a time when the Church was all about keeping up appearances and whitewashed expectations, Rich's voice opened the door for people to be real—to confess that their lives were far from picture perfect. He knew the key to being truly real was the fundamental understanding that even though we have sinned, our Father is watching and waiting "to see the crying boys come running back to His arms" as he wrote in the song "Growing Young."[8]

But things have changed dramatically in the Church over the past couple of decades, and the door to authenticity that Rich helped unlock has been unhinged.

When the pendulum swung towards the law, we realized we could not stand up under the weight of legalism, of simply abiding by the rules. *But wait—there's grace!* Still, under the liberty of grace we sometimes forget the call to righteousness; we become so proud of being a hot mess that we live however, do whatever, whenever, because grace covers it all. Make no mistake—grace does cover us, but grace is not a license to sin or to condone that which does not align with God's Word.

When we run back to God we grow and mature in grace, and then we are better able to help those struggling alongside us. We, as the Church, can help make the distinction in our culture that while it is natural to *struggle with* sin—we all do—we can't *continue in* sin. Accepting sin in the name of "tolerance" is not freedom. First John 5:4 says, "Everyone born of God overcomes the world" (NIV). We cannot overcome what we condone.

Rich's lyrics are full of struggle, full of grace, and full of God's righteousness. They strike a beautiful balance between owning up to sin and falling on the grace of God.

I am eternally grateful for his voice in all its beauty and poetry, and for his friendship—*though we were strangers, still I loved him.*

You see, to love God means that we keep His commands, and His commands don't weigh us down. Everything that has been fathered by God overcomes the corrupt world. This is the victory that has conquered the world: our faith.

1 JOHN 5:3–4

[God's] attention and affection was not won by the attractive and the beautiful—His glance and His love made things and people attractive and beautiful.

RICH MULLINS

CHAPTER 24

GLIMMERS OF GRACE

Ian Morgan Cron

---

*When the imitation of Christ does not mean to live
a life like Christ, but to live your life as authentically
as Christ lived His, then there are many ways
and forms in which a man can be a Christian.*

HENRI NOUWEN

"Art is a wound turned into light." That's what the twentieth-century French painter Georges Braque wrote, and he was right. When artists share their brokenness, it illuminates grace. It creates the natural climate in which the possibility of redemption can reveal itself. We inspire hope when we bravely put on display our fallenness for the world to see.

I never met Rich, but from what friends who knew him have told me, he was prone to melancholy. He was exquisitely attuned to all that was wrong with the world. His music and lyrics have a plaintive quality to them at times. He clearly felt like an exile in the world, a person who paced the cage. Like Brennan Manning and Henri Nouwen, Rich was a "wounded healer." Lord knows we need these people. Wounded people know best how to apply the healing balm to the rest of the world's pain.

In many churches today, you hear language like, "We're sinners, but thankfully God loves us." So the language of, "Let's be authentic," and "Let's be real about our wounds," and "Oh thank goodness for grace," is heard everywhere, but what you actually hear in the background is the choir quietly singing, "*But try harder!*" I suspect Rich would have had little patience for such shame-based mixed messaging.

The truth is, Christianity isn't something you *do* so much as it's something that *gets done to you*. For many of us, our striving is more a pursuit of golden rule suburban respectability than true holiness. While there's nothing wrong with trying to be a good citizen or a morally upright person, this isn't the good news of the gospel. Again, I didn't know Rich, but if his lyrics are any indication, he would have fought this distortion of the Good News.

Sometimes Rich echoes the Catholic monk Thomas Merton. Rich once said, "I would imagine that nothing would be more important than becoming fully who you were supposed to be. You know what I mean? For me, that's what salvation is all about."

When I hear people say, "I just want to be like Jesus," I think, *God doesn't need another Jesus. What God wants is for us to become fully ourselves, and by being fully ourselves, we bring glory to God.*

In Thomas Merton's *New Seeds of Contemplation*, he says, "How does a horse bring glory to God? By being a horse. How does a tree bring glory to God? By being a tree." Human beings are the only creatures on this earth who have the choice to be themselves or to pretend to be someone other than who we genuinely are. Our task is to slough off the illusory self that we wear to deceive ourselves and the world about the nature of our true condition.

At the risk of being cynical, I've seen plenty of pastors (and I've been one, so I count myself among the sinners) take off one suit of clothes to "get real," only to discover another suit of clothes underneath—a falsely self-aware false self who's pretending not to be a false self! Again, I'm sure Rich wouldn't have had much time for this kind of dissembling.

I also think that if Rich were still alive, his political and social positions would be in conflict with the views mainstream evangelicals cling to today. He would have a more progressive theology towards people who the church has historically marginalized. Regardless of whom we are, all any of us can can do is park ourselves in the river of grace where the current runs swiftest, where we can let God do for us what we can't do for ourselves.

Grace does the heavy lifting. That's the gospel. All we can do is make ourselves available to the Spirit and the often imperceptible work of God. It takes a lot of courage.

For it's by God's grace that you have been saved. You receive it through faith. It was not our plan or our effort. It is God's gift, pure and simple. You didn't earn it, not one of us did, so don't go around bragging that you must have done something amazing. For we are the product of His hand, heaven's poetry etched on lives, created in the Anointed, Jesus, to accomplish the good works God arranged long ago.

EPHESIANS 2:8–10

CHAPTER 25

SURRENDER . . .
THE DIVINE PERMISSION

The hardest part of being a Christian is surrendering.
That is where the real struggle happens.

RICH MULLINS

To speak out loud the prayer "God, do for me what I cannot do for myself" requires an immense amount of humility in surrender. And surrender is anything but natural. To acquiesce one's own agenda in order to participate in the greater good requires a concerted decision doused with perspective and humility.

Throughout world history, and in the context of our own life experience, we have seen the gracious benefits of the willingness to surrender. When we lay down our weapons and kneel down at the table of God's completely inclusive communion, the conversation of our lives truly begins—not just for our earthly tenure but for our eternal stay.

Surrender's definition often gets entangled with the modern implications of being submissive (which, when skewed, can enable oppression). But submission within healthy parameters—or within divine permission—advances genuine freedom.

The privilege of surrender is the liberation to simply (though often self-complicatedly) let go. When we finally relinquish our obsessions, our pride, our white-knuckled need to control, we unbind the chains and unlock the door to our true potential, benefitting not only ourselves but also our entire circumference of community. This is the surrender Rich spoke and sang about so often within his lifetime—truly letting go.

At first glance, this may read like some New Age holistic hubbub, but I think surrender is our most intimidating spiritual challenge.

For those of us who practice a particular religion, this contrary relationship with surrender is often defined as "sin." The Catechism of the Catholic Church in 1849 describes sin as "an offense against reason, truth, and right conscience; it is failure in genuine love for God and neighbor caused by a perverse attachment to certain goods. It wounds the nature of man and injures human solidarity."

Sin is much more than a perpetuation of some self-condescending singing of "a wretch like me." In tandem with surrender, the confession of our sins is a release of our shame. Yes, sin is the shortcoming, and often shortsighted-ness of our humanity, but, with awareness and disclosure, we receive the divine permission to transform from who we are presently to who we have been created to be forever. And we have been created well, very well.

I believe our behavior, no matter how abhorrent, could never capture the essence of who we are, nor could any achievement, no matter how glorious, fully charac-terize how much we are loved. So give it up, my friend. The shame you carry from those relationships and circum-stances that were in and out of your control—hand it over. The trophies you worked so hard to earn in order to obtain favor and acceptance from your peers, your family, from yourself—lay them down. They are not who you are.

Through the practice of surrender we discover the stunning perspective of heaven—we are beloved by God.

Once we have overcome our own desire to be elevated, our own desire to be recognized, our own desire to be independent and all those things that we value because we are Americans and we are part of this American culture, once we have overcome that struggle, then God can use us as a part of His body to accomplish what the body of Christ was left here to accomplish.

RICH MULLINS

CHAPTER 26

REFLECTIONS ON RICH

by Mitch McVicker

*Look at us all—we are all of us lost and in all
of our different ways of pretending, we all fool ourselves
into the very same hell. Look at the cross—we are all
of us loved and one God meets us all at the point
of our common need and brings to all of us—
all of us who will let Him—salvation.*

RICH MULLINS

I have no memory of what happened that night.

We had been recording music in Elgin, Illinois. Rich was producing my first album, and after four straight weeks in the studio we loaded up in his 1995 Jeep Wrangler to drive through the night to Wichita, Kansas, where we would perform the first concert of Rich's fall tour the following day.

The concert never took place.

One week later, I awoke from a coma. Though the hospital room was sterile-clean, it smelled like bruises and bandages and blood. I asked the doctor, "Where is Rich?" He told me that we had been in a single-car accident and Rich had been killed. In my drug-induced state, I just shook my head. *No. No. No.* My head injury had me slipping in and out of consciousness, drifting between a dreamlike la-la land and reality. Eventually, I was able to put enough pieces together to realize that life as I had known it would never be the same.

Rich and I had been working together for a few years. We were roommates in a simple, some might call "junky," house trailer on the edge of the Navajo Reservation in New Mexico. We lived just "across the wash" from the mission school where Rich was hoping to teach Navajo children music. We spent our weeks participating in the mission's activities and getting acclimated to Navajo culture. We led retreats, built "hogans,"[9] and ate a lot of fry bread and mutton stew. On the weekends, we toured the country performing concerts. I would strum my guitar and sing harmony while Rich sang his famous storyteller songs. In the middle of the concert, Rich would ask me to play some of my own songs. He was pushing me towards becoming an artist.

He graciously included me in his whirlwind song-writing practices—his mind racing through the entirety of a song, already on to the next idea while I would remain hung up on a single word, line, or stanza. He was sensitive to the song's moment yet in the same breath he would draw from past experiences. His creativity was a hauntingly beautiful thing to behold. I know no better songwriter, anywhere . . . ever.

He held on tightly to his identity as Jesus's kid, and he had a firm hold on his place in God's kingdom. Because of this, Rich was not interested in becoming "successful" or trying to make himself significant. If some element of fame developed as a by-product of living out his identity, then fine, but he was most assuredly unconcerned and unimpressed by commercial success.

During soundcheck before a church concert in Vancouver, the church's pastor approached Rich. He was concerned about Rich's appearance. Rich was wearing hole-riddled jeans and a frayed sweater worn at the elbows, and the pastor was worried, so he said to Rich, "Some of the church's saints might be offended by the way you look." Rich stared at him blankly without saying a word. We left the building and drove around so Rich could smoke and think. When we returned, Rich went onstage and played the concert dressed as he was.

Though Rich was not into material things—in fact, he was often offended by them—he was an admitted experience junkie. He was always excited to visit the shiny, "consumerville" sections of cities when we traveled. Once, as we drove through one of these glitzy commercialized areas of Albuquerque, Rich looked over at me, and with tears in his eyes he said, "The things of this world just don't satisfy, do they?" Rich was able to live simply because he wasn't ensnared by this world's materialistic trappings.

Rich was determined to live in the kingdom of God.

When I was recovering from being in a coma and its associated brain trauma, as well as collapsed lungs and broken bones that would require me to relearn processes I had come to take for granted—like eating, drinking, walking, and talking—I realized Rich was really gone. The hole he left was made bigger by little things. Years went by before I could go to a movie or read a book without feeling an immediate impulse to tell Rich that he, too, should check it out.

Nothing made sense. *Why was Rich taken? Why was I alive? Why God, why?* But I don't know if God is as concerned as much with making sense of our tough stuff as being our friend through the tough stuff. And as God molds and constructs us through hardships, we become more of the person God created us to be in the very beginning—we become ourselves.

Witnessing Rich's acceptance of God's grace as he lived was stunningly sacred. I long to accept God's grace in the same manner so that it might spill over into the songs I sing, the words I speak, and the life I live.

Rich and I lived life, together. I experienced him at his best, I saw him at his worst, and I lived beside him in the middle ground of the magnificent mundane of everyday stuff—and I am all the better for it.

We have many enemies—people who reject the cross of the Anointed. . . . Their minds are fixed on the things of this world. They are doomed. But we are citizens of heaven, exiles on earth waiting eagerly for a Liberator, our Lord Jesus the Anointed, to come and transform these humble, earthly bodies into the form of His glorious body by the same power that brings all things under His control.

PHILIPPIANS 3:18–21

Love GOD, your God. Walk in his ways. Keep his commandments, regulations, and rules so that you will live, really live, live exuberantly, blessed by GOD.

DEUTERONOMY 30:16 MSG

CHAPTER 27

THE POLITICS OF PRAYER

*For a long time I believed that there would be
political solutions, because growing up in America,
you endure several political campaigns and these people
make promises and they say, "We will do this
and we will do that," and you believe them
because you don't know any better.*

RICH MULLINS

Every four years America hosts a national circus widely known as the presidential race. Square in the middle of the latest political barnstorm, with the country hyper-focused on the candidates, the issues, and the nonstop campaigning, my hometown hosted a prayer rally. On the state capitol steps. My inner skeptic was in full swing.

Oh, I believe in the soul-centering power of prayer,

and I want to join the fellowship of saints and sinners praying whenever possible. At the heart of most corporate worship occasions is a trustworthy desire to unite under the influence of Jesus as we verbalize our requests and pleas. But it seems in today's culture wars, everything is politicized. It's tiring for us all, and it is infecting our pulpits and our pews.

But having ulterior motives of a professional variety, I attended. Always susceptible to the charismatic energy of a crowd, I slipped in alongside the thousands assembled and shouldered up to detect—albeit with more cynicism than discernment—if this space set aside for community invocation would invoke more prayer or more politics.

Well, who would have thought? After only a few minutes of his keynote address, the speaker, a famous preacher, asked each person in the crowd to grab the hands of the people standing beside them (mostly strangers). Then he made one simple request: to pray, and to pray out loud.

As the outdoor amphitheater began to chorus with the appeals of the crowd, I could barely formulate even one word. For in that moment there were no doctors, no educators, no pastors or marketing gurus or musicians or politicians. In that moment, there were just us—people with hearts and feelings and hopes and sadness. Restored lives and broken lives in the same room.

And you know what? We didn't begin appealing for a

certain outcome in the election. Our pleas were not focused on any one issue or argument. We weren't petitioning for or against anything or anyone, and for a brief moment, we weren't watching the television ticker or checking our news feeds. We had one simple yet sweeping supplication: *Your will be done on earth as it is in heaven.*

May this expression resonate off our lips over and over until it not only shapes our prayers, but more so until it changes our minds, our eyes, our mouths, our ears, our hands, our feet, and our hearts.

"Your kingdom come. Your will be done on earth as it is in heaven" (Matthew 6:10 NKJV).

What makes humility so desirable is the marvelous thing it does to us; it creates in us a capacity for the closest possible intimacy with God.

MONICA BALDWIN

I thank God now for Richard Nixon and for Gerald Ford and for all those people who betrayed any confidence that the American people could have in their government, who said that the leadership of this country is not accountable to the people who elect them, and who made so clear what we now know that no government works, and I wanted the government to work. . . .

Someday God will destroy injustice. Someday there will be a judgment, and because we have a loving and a forgiving Father, maybe we'll survive it.

RICH MULLINS[10]

CHAPTER 28

BEWILDERED CURIOSITY

Ashley Cleveland

I don't think you read the Bible to know truth.
I think you read the Bible to find God,
and we encounter Him there. Paul says that
the Scriptures are God's breath and I kind of go,
"Wow. So let's breathe this as deeply as possible."

RICH MULLINS

I have completely stopped petitioning. Well, not completely. Every once in a while, I send up a flare, but I decided that I just talk too much.

When I really dig into the Gospels, I don't think I really know this Jesus. Some of the things He said were so puzzling to me. I just did not get it. I'm not a dummy. I'm pretty steeped in Scripture. But I may have been a little too "churched." So, I have been listening.

I am terrible at it so far. My prayer life consists of reading the Psalms, thanking God, and then just sitting there and listening. I really do believe that God speaks to us. The best word He ever gave to us was Jesus, and Jesus is God's word to the world, so if I will just sit, then I can hear something—and if I don't hear anything, somehow I am fed. It is this uncanny alchemy of just *presence*.

I was in a staunchly reformed conservative church when I started having some theological questions. I kept asking these questions in this particular class at my church. No one ever answered them, so I just kept asking. I am a lot like Rich in that. I was not trying to disturb the peace. I genuinely had questions I was wrestling with, but I think what I was really wanting was a vast concession to mystery.

I read this really beautiful excerpt about the difference between Mary and John the Baptist's father, Zechariah. The difference between Mary and Zechariah was genuine inquiry and scoffing inquiry. They both asked the same question of God, and one was so consumed she sang out the Magnificat and the other was made mute. I think, *I don't want to be in that group.* As far as I can tell, questions are welcome.

A lot of my questions do not have to be answered because the only one that really matters was answered a long time ago, but I am still going to ask them. I want to draw close. I want to further acquaint myself with this

God who has consumed me, like Jeremiah, "in my heart as a burning fire."[11] I want to know Him, and I am very aware that I only know a tiny bit. I have heard "wonder" described as this "bewildered curiosity," which is bound up in the fear of the Lord—so the fear of the Lord is wonder.

I will be posing questions until the day I die, and I would fight for anyone to be able to ask their questions. One of our greatest gifts is free will. It's a terrible gift, but it is a gift. It allows us this curiosity that Rich showed us over and over. Keep asking.

But when I tell myself, I'll never mention Your name or speak for You again, it's no use. *The word of God burns in my heart; it is like fire in my bones. I try to hold it all in, but I cannot.*

JEREMIAH 20:9

There is the unsettling element of perplexity, but add to it the element of curiosity, and, voilà, wonder!

WILLIAM P. BROWN

CHAPTER 29

THE SPEECH
OF THE ETERNAL

Joy and sorrow are this ocean
and in their every ebb and flow
Now the Lord a door has opened that
all hell could never close.
Here I'm tested and made worthy,
tossed about but lifted up
In the reckless raging fury
that they call the love of God.

RICH MULLINS

My first visual of Rich was from a music video filmed in Ireland. With his hands burrowed in a black, knee-length peacoat, the dark-haired (and a bit disheveled) thirty-something musician stood along the imposing cliffs of the

Emerald Isle's brooding seascapes while he peered upward at a camera and sang the now-iconic lyrics to his song "The Color Green." The visual tribute to the song's Irish overtones still stun me when I watch it today, twenty-five years after its inception. But the pairing of the imagery of the mystical Irish seas with the grandeur of Rich's music was perfectly enchanting.

There is a rhythm to water, a push and pull that resonates deep down in our bodies, and deep down in our spirits. That video captured it.

Adventurers wander cross-country to spend a few days on the West Coast, burrowing their feet into the Pacific Ocean's soft-grain sands and soaking up every drop of brilliant optimism Southern California's perpetual sunshine will permit. Or they point their compass due East to overlook the moody waters bordering the Carolinas, finding moments of peace and quiet in the brooding cadence of Big Pond Atlantic.

From sea to shining sea, travelers and soul searchers find solace in the steadiness of the surf. Compelled by the sea, we are both awe-inspired by its peaceful ebb-and-flow and scared silly by its tormenting power.

Describing our draw to big bodies of water, a good friend of mine says it must be "because the voice of the Lord is upon the waters" (a paraphrase of Psalm 29).

Growing up in church, I'd hear congregants or

ministers or youth pastors talk about hearing God's voice. I was always curious as to how this great, eternal Creator's speech might sound. And then I would feel insecure that I had never heard Him speak. Or had I?

"The voice of the Eternal echoes over the great waters; God's magnificence roars like thunder" (Psalm 29:3). And I wade a bit deeper into the waves, eagerly eavesdropping as the waters brew a fantastic storm.

"The Eternal's voice shatters the cedars. . . . The Voice of the Eternal rumbles through the wilderness" (Psalm 29:5, 8). And I walk farther into the thicket, tuning my senses to the chorus of the forest's towering pines.

"The Eternal's voice brings life from the doe's womb" (Psalm 29:9). And I grin at the everyday discoveries of children, wide-eyed and wondering at the world and all it gives and takes away.

Perhaps the transcription of God's tongue is too unwieldy to ever be contained by syllables and speech. But if we open our ears, our eyes, our hearts, our spirits, I do believe He is speaking. Sometimes in a whisper. Sometimes in a "reckless raging fury." But always speaking. Wondrously. And I think He has some splendid things to say.

God dwells in His creation and is everywhere indivisibly present in all His works. He is transcendent above all His works even while He is immanent within them.

A. W. Tozer

CHAPTER 30

CHANGE THE WORLD

David Leo Schultz

We didn't know what love was 'til He came
And He gave love a face and He gave love a name.

RICH MULLINS

Study the lives of the great saints—men and women like Julian of Norwich, Saint Francis of Assisi and his notable early disciple, Saint Clare of Assisi, late twentieth-century theologian Brennan Manning, and yes, musician and lyricist Rich Mullins—and it seems in their deepest efforts to connect to God, they share three common denominators.

They valued the inward, contemplative life in exchange for an outward busy life. They quietly asked themselves the important question, *What if I accepted Jesus's call to follow Him literally, and seriously?*

They were experiential, perceiving experience as a more powerful conduit for the Holy Spirit to transform their hearts and lives than, say, reason or a heavy, theological facts-based sermon. They fell head-over-heels, ridiculously and foolishly in love with Christ as a response to God being head-over-heels, ridiculously and foolishly in love with us.

And lastly, none of them were afraid, as Brennan said, to admit that Christianity is for "the inconsistent, unsteady disciples whose cheese is falling off their cracker." Or as Saint Francis said, "I have been all things unholy. If God can work through me, He can work through anyone."

The life Rich Mullins lived was louder than the songs he sang. He was keenly aware—maybe beautifully *un*aware—that to change the world you only need one thing—love. For God *is* love.

Our world has remained the same since Genesis 3, since the beginning. We are still in need of redemption, recovery, and resuscitation of the heart. Or to translate it into my native Indiana vernacular, "Our world needs a changin'!" And this happens when someone walks a different way than religious gluttons or the spiritually empty, a person who isn't following a play-it-safe or commercialized, "this is good for business" kind of Christianity.

The world is changed by someone who follows the

loving footsteps of Jesus. Someone like Saint Clare and Saint Francis and Brennan . . . and Rich.

So, like them, will you answer the barbaric cry to literally and seriously follow Jesus, the Christ? Will you foolishly fall head-over-heels in love with Someone you cannot see with human eyes but only with eyes of the Spirit? Are you ready to surrender, to let go of the game of pretending to be perfect and be brave enough to, as Jesus said, "lose . . . your life for My sake"? (Matthew 10:39).

If you do this, you too might change the world.

I have been crucified with the Anointed One—I am no longer alive—but the Anointed is living in me; and whatever life I have left in this failing body I live by the faithfulness of God's Son, the One who loves me and gave His body on the cross for me.

GALATIANS 2:20

I deeply feel that once we come into the covenant through Jesus, once we have come through the way with Him, that God really sees Christ when He looks at us. And the sin in our life really is buried with Christ. . . .

And the work of the Spirit is just to get us to catch up with what has already happened.

RICH MULLINS[12]

CHAPTER 31

WORRY INTO WORSHIP

I take comfort in knowing that it was the shepherds
to whom the angels appeared when they announced
Christ's birth. Invariably throughout the course of history,
God has appeared to people on the fringes.
It's nice to find theological justification for your quirks.

RICH MULLINS

We all wrestle with fear. We all get scared. Sure, some of us are less skittish than others, but being afraid—of cancer, of the government, of the weather, of our finances, of each other—has gradually become our cultural norm. We wear anxiety as a badge of honor, as if the unmanageability of our mind and emotions is a status symbol. Maybe we have glorified fear because, honestly, we are scared to death of it.

This is one of the reasons I am drawn to music. The

rhythm of a verse and crescendo of a chorus generously move our hearts beyond the angst of daily living towards the contentment of eternal life. The strains of song speak or sing out our doubts, until our souls harmonize with faith. For many of us, Rich's music provided a restorative relief. His songs administered an antidote for our apprehensions. Music changes the most nervous Nellies into people of peace.

> *And there were in the same country shepherds abiding in the field, keeping watch over their flock by night. And, lo, the angel of the Lord came upon them, and the glory of the Lord shone round about them: and they were sore afraid.*
>
> LUKE 2:8–9 KJV

I'm not sure how "sore" translates, but it sounds to me like the spotlighted shepherds were so filled with fear that it physically hurt. I get that. Don't you? I have been stunned by panic before, so confused with worry that the task of getting dressed and leaving home felt like a monumental achievement, as if with even the most basic aspiration to be a full-functioning, responsible adult I was failing.

> *And the angel said unto them, Fear not.*
>
> LUKE 2:10 KJV

I have a hunch that these celestial creatures didn't merely speak this quelling chorus into the atmosphere, they must have sung it. And in the current of a heavenly melody the apprehension building inside of the shepherds' hearts was transformed from a quivering anxiety into a glorious anticipation. Under the cover of night came a great light, and worry was turned into worship. From fear, faith was born.

"For, behold, I bring you good tidings of great joy, which shall be to all people. For unto you is born this day in the City of David a Saviour, which is Christ the Lord" (Luke 2:10–11 KJV). He is here. God, present with us. We no longer have to be afraid. Amen.

If we still ourselves, if we let [God] calm us, focus us, equip us for the day . . . then He will give us hope—hope that stretches us (where worry bent us) and faith—faith that sustains us (where greed smothered us) and love—love that is at the bottom of our deepest desires, the loss of which is at the root of all our fears.

RICH MULLINS

CHAPTER 32

REFLECTIONS ON RICH

Marita Meinerts Albinson

We all want to be useful to God. Well, it's no big deal—
God can use anybody. God used Nebuchadnezzar.
God used Judas Iscariot. . . . I would much rather
have God want me than have God use me.

RICH MULLINS

Growing up within the walls of a conservative Baptist church in rural Minnesota tends to shape a young girl's heart in a certain way. Reverent love for Jesus and for the Word of God was central to our weekly worship services. Yet some practiced orthodoxies seemed to suggest a fixed faith—one where you find the "right" answers, then sit down and sit still. But even at a tender age, I knew that my faith had energy and the need to move with fluidity and dynamism. Believing the power of music incorporated this faith that could inspire and heal, I moved to Nashville after college to pursue a career in supporting and promoting contemporary Christian music.

On my very first day of employment I met David McCracken, a sweet and loving brotherly figure who worked mere feet away from me at Reunion Records, the music company where already-legendary artists like Michael W. Smith and Amy Grant walked the halls. So did Richard Wayne Mullins—bare footed with a bared heart and a barely there, childlike grin.

Because of my role in marketing and communications at the label, my initial encounters with Rich were based on business. But through the generous and multiplying friendship of David, I was brought into authentic community with these two gentle souls. It was that tenderness of heart that made Rich, his words, and his music so magnetic—not just for fans around the world, but for *me*. Rich's liberal dose of love, poured over the truth of Scripture (Rich studied the Bible and knew it well), motivated me to move toward grace and freedom in my faith journey—a truth not always welcomed in my more conservative upbringing.

For a number of years before he died, I traveled from coast to coast with Rich as his road manager. This afforded me the opportunity to experience literally hundreds of

Rich's concerts. The vulnerability that he shared through his lyrics, poetry, stories, and personal revelations—both in live performances as well as in his recordings—allowed the light of Christ to shine through the cracks of his self-criticism and insecurities, a trait often revealed in the more sensitive and open of hearts.

Hearts shaped by sensitivity and openness often draw people in because they more easily offer a place of recognition and refuge for wounded wanderers and seekers. Sensitive hearts provide a soft place to land for those brave enough to approach. I certainly felt that magnetic pull toward Rich's authenticity and the raw talent that allowed him to put words and music to the stirrings of my heart, yet I also observed that the owner of such a heart can often have challenges with self-love and care. I find it a bit ironic, if not unfair, that the tenderhearted readily extend grace and insight to fellow sojourners, yet are quick to find fault and imperfection in themselves. Perhaps it is because such sensitivity to the human condition gives us eyes to see the needs of others with relative clarity while the darkness in ourselves remains under-lit.

Rich's willingness to reveal his flaws and blemishes gave others permission to do the same, and I believe that is why his words and ideas continue to resonate with so many. It is mysterious and mystical when human hearts and minds begin to flower from a tightly wound bud into a fluttering full bloom because of being exposed to and nourished by the light . . . the light of love, the light of truth, the light of Jesus.

Anyone who loves a fellow believer is living in the light and does not cause others to stumble.

1 JOHN 2:10 NLT

CHAPTER 33

A CONVERSATION
WITH SHANE CLAIBORNE

The poor, the disenfranchised, people and groups who were on the fringes of society—those people had Rich's attention. And for him, this seemed to be a direct connection to the gospel. Shane Claiborne consistently works with these people groups.

Q: You have spent the last ten years supporting and developing a very early church–type community outside of Philadelphia. Do you connect with this everyman gospel Rich was so compelled by?

Shane Claiborne: What I came to see—and Rich helped with this—is that when you look at Jesus from the moment He's born until He is a refugee, in the middle of a genocide where Herod is killing all the little boys in the land, until He dies on the cross, convicted, executed, publicly shamed, buried in a borrowed tomb, it is the most beautiful act of divine solidarity. God leaves all the comfort of heaven and moves in with us, comes in the most vulnerable expressions of humanity possible. I heard somebody say, "It's great that Jesus wasn't too worried about His comfort and safety or He would have never left heaven."

What is beautiful is that in Jesus, God puts skin on and moves into the neighborhood with us, and comes from a place where people said nothing good could come from. After living in Kensington, Pennsylvania, for twenty years, that means a lot to me. My neighborhood had been so stigmatized that people around Philadelphia called Kensington "the bad lands." I always correct them. "You better be careful. That's exactly what they said of Nazareth—nothing good could come from there."

What we see in the gospel is this nearness to the poor and to the most vulnerable. Even Mary, as she cries out in Luke's Gospel, the mighty are cast from their thrones, the lowly are lifted, the hungry are filled with good things, the rich are sent away empty.[13] This gospel is the absolute contradiction of the patterns of the world that call us to move away from suffering, the kind of sprawl that pulls us out of neighborhoods where there's high crime or people that don't look like us, and yet the gravity of the gospel pulls us towards the suffering, towards the most broken and forsaken corners of our world. That's what Rich embodied and believed so beautifully.

Q: Culture doesn't exactly set us up for success in this endeavor, so how do we embody this gospel mindset?

Shane: Community helps. Rich lived in community. He didn't just have a band, he had these ragamuffins that made music together, but music was just a part of their life together. Then he moved into this idea of the Kid Brothers of St. Frank—this almost neo-monastic following of Jesus inspired by Saint Francis of Assisi.

In the Bible, we're called to community. We're created in the image of God and that reflects community to us: Father, Son, and Spirit. When the first humans are created, God doesn't pronounce it as "really good" until they are together, helping each other. The story of Exodus is a story of a liberation community, of slaves being liberated. Jesus modeled community for us. Wherever two or three of you gather in my name, I'm with you.[14] The disciples are sent out in pairs. As we try to follow Jesus and seek first the kingdom of God, which is so upside down from the values of our world, it is so important that we need other people—what sociologists call a "plausibility structure." We need a critical mass to help us swim against the stream.

Community is about surrounding ourselves with people who help us become better. They help us become more like Jesus. Community is about surrounding ourselves with the people that remind us of who we want to be. If you want to be generous, hang out with generous people. If you want to be more courageous, more of a risk-taker, hang out with people that are fearless. If you hang out with cynical people, they make you cynical. If you hang out with narcissistic people and watch the Kardashians, you're going to be a narcissist.

In my own story, from starting "The Simple Way," to going to India and working with Mother Teresa, to going to Iraq and Afghanistan during the war, to going to jail, all of these things have been done in the context of community. This is not a lone ranger kind of thing—it's about a discipleship that happens in the context of community. I have received courage that would have been impossible to call up on my own.

Q: From the time you spent with Mother Teresa in Calcutta, and through the communal heartbeat of The Simple Way in Kensington, you have coined a phrase, "consistent life ethic." This promotes a holistic, kingdom of God lifestyle in every area of life. Rich only allowed himself an average man's salary, and gave the rest to others, I think in an effort to afford a "consistent life ethic." Millions were potentially given away to help infrastructure the finances of other individuals and organizations. As disciples of Jesus, what does a "consistent life ethic" mean?

Shane: The way Rich handled his money provoked my own imagination around finances. John Wesley did the same thing. He lived on so little. Eventually the Wesleys generated massive amounts of money and still lived off of that little living stipend that he had committed to, like Rich.

I capped off my income many years ago, and still live off of a living stipend similar to my neighbors and my community mates. People sometimes think that's very virtuous, but like John Wesley said, "When I have any money, I get rid of it as quickly as possible, lest it find a way into my heart."

A consistent life ethic is one of the most important frameworks for us today. It's new to a lot of evangelicals, but the idea of a consistent life ethic, the sanctity of life, the "seamless garment," has been a part of Catholic ethical teaching—it's Mennonite. The framework of it says every person is created in the image of God. So every time someone's life is taken, or someone's dignity is squashed, we lose a little of that image in the world. So the Author of life stands on the side of life, and stands consistently against death.

Rich had some really radical critiques in some of his less popular songs—that's part of why I miss him. I think he would have been a voice that proclaimed and embodied a consistent ethic of life. . . . He was on the very edge of that prophetic critique.

What I love about Mother Teresa, too, is that to be pro-life did not just mean wearing a T-shirt that says "Abortion is murder," but it meant taking in a fourteen-year-old girl that was pregnant who didn't know how in the world she would raise her kid. It meant taking in kids abandoned in train stations. She was known for her passion against abortion, but she was just as passionate against the death penalty, and that meant calling governors the week of execution and saying, "I'm praying for you. Do what Jesus would have you do. Show mercy. Blessed are the merciful for they will be shown mercy." She was a holy agitator.

When we think of our political options, there's not a party or a candidate that has a real consistent ethic of life. But the framework is resonating with a lot of people right now. In a world with so much violence and so much working against life, I long to see more Christians that are saying we stand on the side of life and the side of love. When we think of evangelicals, people think of us as people who have been blessing bombs and celebrating guns and all those things. I think we have to change that.

Q: Isn't this the framework of eternity? If we are eternal beings—eternity is already alive and working in and through us. When we work on the side of life, as Christ's followers, isn't that our connection to eternity— this bigger kingdom perspective already alive in us?

Shane: For sure. The problem is we've separated the thin states of this life and the next. Jesus is constantly saying, "Today's the day of salvation. The kingdom is now." This is eternal life: to know God. It's not something you wait for when you die. But for many of us in the Church, we've been so focused on heaven that we've forgotten earth. Jesus is praying that the kingdom would come, "on earth as it is in heaven." Many people have said that many Christians are so heavenly minded that they're not much earthly good.

Some of what we've done is use our faith as a ticket into heaven and permission to ignore the world around us. So we tell people there's life after death, but folks are asking, "Is there life before death?" "Doesn't your gospel have anything to speak into our current reality?" That's where Jesus shines so brightly.

Rich knew that Jesus didn't come just to prepare us to die. Jesus came to teach us how to live, and how to love— and how to bring heaven down.

Top: Rich with his dad and mom, John and Neva Mullins.
Bottom: Rich's boyish grin.

PART 3

TROUBADOUR

Longing for Home

So go out and live real good and I promise you'll get beat up real bad. But, in a little while after you're dead, you'll be rotted away anyway. It's not gonna matter if you have a few scars. It will matter if you didn't live.[1]

RICH MULLINS

Rich jokingly referred to himself as the "Daggone Star," so his friend
David McCracken gave him a "star" shirt.

Song of a Troubadour
(I'd Rather Be with You)

Well the whitewater wanders through those Hoosier hills
The river runs right on
And the moon rises over the furrowed fields
And this Greyhound rolls along.
But it won't take me where I would rather be
Where my heart leads me to
It won't take me where I would rather be
'Cause I'd rather be with You.
As the turning wheels take me over prairie miles
The window frames the stars
Outside here the mile markers sail on by
And this highway reaches far.
I spent most of my life running away from the things I needed
I spent most of my time being too proud to pray
But pride won't get me next to You.
And the neon lights flashing on those city signs
So many miles to go
And the billboards send messages to the blind
Just to keep them on this road.
But it won't take me where I would rather be
Where my heart leads me to
It won't take me where I would rather be
'Cause I'd rather be with You.

Lyrics by Rich Mullins, Phil Naish, and Lowell Alexander[2]

Backstage with Ragamuffin band member Jimmy Abegg, 1993.

Part 3

INTRODUCTION

Rich was infatuated—or more accurately, compelled—to communicate from an eternal mindset. He continuously chipped away at as much of the puzzle of infinity as he could while still being bound by the finite framework of his mortality. His shared meditations resurrected in us an internal, eternal awareness long-lain dormant by the distraction of our daily routines and ambitions. His fixation on the reality of heaven was infectious. His discourse about something so unknown was readily accessible because we have the same pinings percolating just beneath the surface of our humanity.

Rich spent his life longing for home.

There is an ache within each of us—a yearning that has yet to be fulfilled, a desire that cannot be fully demonstrated in or assuaged by our current context of body and blood. Though the craving is certain, the terms of our yearning are rather cryptic. These lives we lead are gathered with purpose and tethered with meaning, but the significance of our here and now still lies in the beautiful consequence of the yet to come.

Every painful heartbreak and each surprising joy is not strictly limited to an association with this body, these bones, and this breath. Our soul's insistence is that we have yet to arrive at our home. Our earthly lives are shrouded in feelings of foreignness, some abiding notion that our citizenship far supersedes a zipcode or nationality. We hear a wild call in the distance, howling our most real names, beckoning us to enter into a dimension where we can live, and live free, forever.

For some of us, within these conversations with Rich about death and life we first felt the evocation of eternity. His wasn't so much an eccentric obsession with death (though there may be some truth to that as well). No, Rich was constantly on the hunt for home.

Whether we chose to probe the profound depths of our forever nature or remain on the surface of this human life, the fact remains: before we were even conceived within our mothers' wombs, the extravagance of eternity was alive in us. Rich just helped us remember.

CHAPTER 34

THE BITTERSWEET LONGING

Carolyn Arends

*God lets us struggle and lets us prosper—we don't
all struggle and prosper the same, but we all do
both to some degree. And when we have done enough
to think more highly of ourselves than
we should, God lets us age.*

RICH MULLINS

Rich's work—like Rich himself—was strikingly playful
and hopeful, and yet there's no denying the undercurrents
of sadness running through almost everything he wrote.
Where did they come from?

Some of it was biographical, no doubt—by the time
I met him, Rich had experienced his fair share of highs

and heartbreaks. And some of it had to be genetic—Rich was just wired to feel the full spectrum of emotions at high intensity. When he laughed, he laughed hard; when he was angry, he burned hot. When he loved a book, he was relentless in his conviction that you *had* to read it. He could access a range of feeling—including both joy and sorrow—swiftly and thoroughly.

I would also guess that Rich's facility with sadness was part of his gifting as an artist. He seemed to be consistently in touch with the bittersweet longing that haunts a lot of great literature and art—the exquisite ache best expressed by the German idea of *sehnsucht.*

In his essay *The Weight of Glory,* C. S. Lewis describes *sehnsucht* as:

> The secret also which pierces with such sweetness that when, in very intimate conversation, the mention of it becomes imminent, we grow awkward and affect to laugh at ourselves; the secret we cannot hide and cannot tell, though we desire to do both. We cannot tell it because it is a desire for something that has never actually appeared in our experience. We cannot hide it because our experience is constantly suggesting it, and we betray ourselves like lovers at the mention of a name.

The experience of *sehnsucht* was a part of C. S. Lewis's conversion. It pointed him to the existence of God, because, he reasoned, the longing that so defines human experience must have an ultimate object. For Rich, I suspect, his experience of God infused his work with *sehnsucht,* because he knew firsthand that there was so much more for which to long.

If biographical, genetic, and artistic factors preconditioned Rich Mullins to be a man well acquainted with both joy and sorrow, I believe what sealed the deal in the last years of his life was the fact that Rich's friendship with God drew him into a deep identification with—even a participation *in*—the suffering of Christ. "Blessed are those who mourn,"[3] Jesus once said, when He was providing a list of qualities you find in people who have been invaded by the kingdom of heaven.

Rich's imagination was so saturated by biblical narratives, his life so ravaged by divine encounter, that his heart began to be broken by the things that break the heart of God. Yes, he longed for the winds of heaven, but he also ached for the redemption and restoration of the stuff of earth, and he had the courage to let some of Christ's passion for the world infuse his own.

Do we?

Now, although a fiddle may never be fooled by the folly of human thinking, very much like us, they have pain. Their necks are stiff and their nerves, their strings, are stretched. They feel the friction of the bow and inside their beautiful brown little bodies they have only a little stick called a soundpost and an emptiness that seizes every inch of space—top to bottom, side to side. Their emptiness is for them (as it is for us) a nearly unbearable ache—an ache that is fitted to the shape that makes its tone. And sometimes a fiddle is tempted to fill that void with rags or glass or gold, even knowing that, if it should do that, it would never again resonate the intentions of its fiddler. It would never again be alive with his music. It would dull itself to the exquisite heat of the fiddler's will, the deliberate tenderness of his fingers.

And so, it resists. It resists so that it can respond.

RICH MULLINS

CHAPTER 35

EVIDENCES OF EDEN

Aim at heaven and you will get earth "thrown in":
Aim at earth and you get neither.

C. S. LEWIS

Way back in the 1990s, mail order was a thing. E-mail was strictly sent via heavy IBMs located in college computer "labs"—a dicey noun that seemed to imply with one wrong stroke of the keyboard, the user might suddenly morph into a floppy disk. Before digital music, streaming movies, or instant access to anything other than a dial tone, a consumer would call the seller, recite their credit card number out loud *over the phone*, while some human being copied it on, I don't know, say, a napkin, by hand.

Once the order was placed, you simply, well . . . waited. And waited. And got annoyed. And waited some more.

The footnotes of most order forms read, "Please allow 4–6 weeks for delivery." That's more than a month. One-eighth of an entire year. A thousand-plus hours. Patience was actually a survival mechanism twenty years ago.

I remember as a youngster wishing for time to advance faster. Now, as an adult, I pray for life to just slow down. When I was a younger man, the thought of eternity scared me. It doesn't bother me as much anymore.

My grandfather, Cecil Girard, was eighty-nine years old when he died. In his last decade of this life, I would visit often. Granddad was a very capable man, but as his age advanced and his health diminished he would steady himself by pressing the weight of his balance into the grid-lock of our joined hands. My father is now seventy years old. In only so long, he too will need that steadying hand.

Why does time go by so quickly these days?

Why is it that we are given this construct of one life to live only to embody souls that completely defy the idea? Why does every fiber of our being long for something more whole, yet we continually scrape at this paradigm in a last-ditch effort to salvage our bodies and turn back the clock?

While this perishable frame rages towards life's finish line, evidences of Eden's eternity echoes in our hearts, prodding our souls toward the Garden—toward God, or as Rich would often sing and say, to home. Perhaps we ache for a pause in the hurrying hours and space to soak in life's fleeting moments. The groundwork for eternity was laid in our spirits long before we breathed a single breath.

And I heard a loud voice from the throne saying, "Behold, the dwelling place of God is with man. He will dwell with them, and they will be his people, and God himself will be with them as their God. He will wipe away every tear from their eyes, and death shall be no more, neither shall there be mourning, nor crying, nor pain anymore, for the former things have passed away."

REVELATION 21:3–4 ESV

We cannot live in a world that is not our own, in a world that is interpreted for us by others. An interpreted world is not a home. Part of the terror is to take back our own listening, to use our own voice, to see our own light.

HILDEGARD OF BINGEN

CHAPTER 36

REFLECTIONS ON RICH

Keith Bordeaux

I hope that I would leave a legacy of joy.
A legacy of real compassion. Because I think there
is great joy in real compassion. I don't think that you can
know joy apart from caring deeply about people—
caring enough about people that you actually do something.

RICH MULLINS

Rich and I first met in the spring of 1997 when I attended one of his concerts while working at his booking agency. We ended up hanging out after the show until the early hours of the morning, and he shared with me his heart for Native Americans.

He had moved to the Navajo Nation in New Mexico a couple years prior and was making plans to expand his ministry by starting after-school music programs and summer camps for the Navajo kids. His music career would provide the financial support for the ministry, and he was in the process of assembling a small team to live with him on the reservation and help him implement his vision. This inner-circle community was called "The Kid Brothers of St. Frank." Rich asked if I would join.

A few months later, Rich and I traveled to New Mexico with a few folks from his record label to witness the stunningly beautiful, but economically impoverished, area where the Kid Brothers of St. Frank would be living, to meet some of his Navajo and missionary friends on the reservation, and to hear songs from a new album he was scheduled to record that fall. When I returned from the trip, I immediately turned in my notice to the booking agency; I was going to go work with Rich.

Five days later, he was killed.

The sudden loss of a new mentor, friend, and opportunity was devastating. I was confused and wondered why God had brought me to this point, only to rip the carpet out from underneath me.

A few months after Rich's untimely death, Compassion International posted a job opening for an "Artist Relations Manager." I applied. Rich, and other artists that I knew personally, were spokespeople for Compassion, so I had some familiarity with the organization, but before meeting

Rich, I was focused on a career in artist management. Full-time ministry to the poor was not on my radar, but God explicitly used Rich's compassionate influence on my life to open my eyes and heart to a different path— a path that allows me the privilege of using my talents to extend a helping hand to the poor and give a voice to those without one.

It's true: Sometimes only hindsight allows us to understand the purposes and plans God redeems from the difficulties in our lives. For nearly two decades now, I have worked on behalf of children living in poverty all over the world through Compassion, and this work has been one of the greatest joys of my life. I will always thank God that He used Rich Mullins to divert my path along the way.

Rich is home now and seeing things that we still long to understand. The veil has been lifted. There is no more mystery. He has met St. Francis, the greatest influence on his spiritual life after Christ, at whose feet Rich now sits. For those of us still stuck down here in skin, we are doing our best to walk by faith, love others along the way, and carry hope for our ultimate home—just like Rich did.

To be able to go through the depths with another human being—that is the supreme act of compassion. That is more important than any particular, well thought out, clearly articulated exclamation for the origin of evil and suffering. But it is so much harder to do.

DANIEL J. SIMUNDSON

CHAPTER 37

NOT HOME YET

We've got a little while to go yet in this life,
and it's a scary thing, but don't be afraid. Be of good cheer.
He has overcome the world. And He has chosen
to dwell within us. And we ain't all that big of a deal,
but our Savior is. He will walk with us through this life,
and when it's over, He will raise us up again and take us to
be where He is—not because of what we've done,
but because of who He is, because of the love He has for us.
So go and live in that awareness—love one another,
read your Bible, wash your dishes,
make your bed, and don't be afraid.

RICH MULLINS

Rich's life was occupied by eternal matters. He seemed to endure a pressure on his spirit, a notion of a deeper calling and some transcendental suspicion that the waters we charter in this life are simply skimming the surface of an unfathomable ocean. There is a certain weight of the soul, a steadfast suffering that gives credit to this fundamental feeling that there is more to our reality than merely flesh and bone. It is a terrible, comforting thought—that this time and place is merely a sample for our senses to whet our appetite for an eternity instilled in us by a Creator long before our atoms were sparked by the passion of our parents.

My dad and I connect deeply, especially in spiritual conversation. While still in elementary school, I asked my father if he understood this unexplainable longing, the impression that we are incomplete or not yet whole— of being caught in between who we are and who it feels like we were meant to be. (I also asked if he thought it was strange to be posing existential questions before I even liked girls. He appeared unmoved.) After scouring his memory for a moment, he recollected sitting, also as a boy, on his grandmother's porch under Louisiana's weepy pines feeling the way I felt, and asking her if she understood this undefined emotion we share. She responded, "Of course. We simply aren't home yet."

We live within a self-help, trying-to-never-die era. Longing for something more deep-rooted and basic and soulful than this human archetype can be dismissed as a sappy sentiment—a placebo for our present pains and a baseless hope in a utopian paradise somewhere in the Great Unknown. But as sure as one can be sure, I am certain of living, in some context, forever. Our current understandings are so thoroughly infused with the essence of eternity. There are so many clues, so many breadcrumb trails— so many signs of other dimensions to life. And perhaps the greatest of these signposts is love.

Love probes planes more profound than our worldly state demands. More than physical affection, or a declaration of commitment, love electrifies our very existence, imbuing even our most trivial moments with everlasting significance. More than solving our pain, love bores deep to unearth a context that, rather than eliminating the pain, infuses it with meaning. Along with heavy heartaches, our earthly pilgrimage is punctuated with magnificent joys. We do not simply exist, we, indeed, are living. Love cannot eliminate our hardships, but it will provide the feather bed for us to rest upon while we find the courage, strength, and resource of spirit we didn't even know we possessed.

Love is not a remedy for life. In its very core, love is life. Love is the springboard from which everything was created. It is the significance of everything that has existed, now exists, or will exist. And love is the current that will carry us through to the other side. Until then, "We simply aren't home yet."

So we have no reason to despair. Despite the fact that our outer humanity is falling apart and decaying, our inner humanity is breathing in new life every day. You see, the short-lived pains of this life are creating for us an eternal glory that does not compare to anything we know here. So we do not set our sights on the things we can see with our eyes. All of that is fleeting; it will eventually fade away. Instead, we focus on the things we cannot see, which live on and on.

2 CORINTHIANS 4:16–18

CHAPTER 38

MERCY!

Mark Lee from Third Day

We never understand what we're praying, and God,
in His mercy, does not answer our prayers according
to our understanding, but according to His wisdom.

RICH MULLINS

My first understanding of mercy was not a theological one. For me, it was a dreaded playground game.

For those of you who haven't had the "good fortune" of playing Mercy, you clasp hands with somebody, say "go," and try to twist and contort your opponent's hands in a way that causes enough pain so that they will literally shout, "Mercy!" As you can imagine, Mercy awards the strong, the quick, and the agile. Since I possessed none of those traits as a child, the game brought me more pain and agony than it did fun.

Real life often feels like a game of Mercy. We live in a world that favors those with power. It's a zero sum game, so success comes to the strong at the expense of the weak. The winner dominates, and despite cries for mercy, the loser gets left behind. The stakes are high, and the pain is real. Deep down we know the game is cruel, but we shrug our shoulders and think, *This is how things have always been done.*

But thankfully, God doesn't play by the rules. Instead of fighting power with power, He does something entirely unexpected. He leans in to the poor, weak, and downtrodden and whispers, "Mercy." He sends the "foolish" example of Jesus, who came not to rule and dominate but to suffer and to serve. We deserved death, but Jesus offered eternal life. He didn't give us what we deserve; He gave us mercy.

This is the God we worship.

In the book of Romans, Paul suggests, "In view of God's mercy, to offer your bodies as a living sacrifice, holy and pleasing to God—this is your spiritual act of worship" (12:1 NIV). God looks down mercifully on our broken world, and as we return His gaze, we see that though we deserve death we receive life instead. This causes us to live in a way that says, "God, thank You for what You have done for us," reflecting God's mercy back to Him and to everyone around us.

God has done something foolish and extravagant for

us. In turn, we live our lives out of that same kind of foolishness. Love and grace and compassion replace strength and will and domination. We look out for the weak, the downtrodden, and the least of these. And with God, we shout "Mercy!"

For people who are stumbling toward ruin, the message of the cross is nothing but a tall tale for fools by a fool. But for those of us who are already experiencing the reality of being rescued and made right, it is nothing short of God's power.

1 CORINTHIANS 1:18

Thus the vocation of the baptized person is a simple thing: it is to live from day to day, whatever the day brings, in this extraordinary unity, in this reconciliation with all people and all things, in this knowledge that death has no more power, in this truth of the resurrection. It does not really matter exactly what a Christian does from day to day. What matters is that whatever one does is done in honor of one's own life, given to one by God and restored to one in Christ, and in honor of the life into which all humans and all things are called. The only thing that really matters is to live in Christ instead of death.

WILLIAM STRINGFELLOW

CHAPTER 39

The Open Table

Jonathan Martin

*I am a Christian, not because someone explained
the nuts and bolts of Christianity to me, but because
there were people willing to be nuts and bolts, who through
their explanation of it held it together so that I could
experience it and be compelled by it to obey.*

Rich Mullins

Christian faith, thankfully, is not rooted in abstractions of theology and doctrine, but in the tactile, tangible, ground floor experience of the Lord's table. For followers of Jesus, dogma comes forth out of table practices, not the other way around. What we eat and drink—and how we eat and drink—tells us who God is, and who we are (in that order).

Depending on one's ecclesial tradition, table practices

vary. But regardless of where or how you receive the Lord's supper, I am convinced of two essential realities: One, Christ is somehow, in a way that is past my wildest fathoming, mysteriously present to us when we partake of the meal. Two, I believe that Christ invites any and all kinds of people to His table—so that no one is left out. If the table is not open to all, it is not yet the table of the Lord.

I don't believe any of this for sentimental reasons. The faith of the Gospels is grounded in stories about Jesus, and the central scandal of those stories, in all four Gospels, is the table practice of Jesus. "Why does your teacher eat together with tax collectors and sinners?"[4] the Pharisees ask. The most simple, elemental customs of the religious purity code are upended by Jesus's far-from-customary practice of sharing meals eyeball-to-eyeball with those who were considered ceremonially unclean. This "scandal" was not lost on the early Christian communities to whom these Gospels were written. These accounts were passed down with the formation of particular people, in particular places, in mind—the intention was that the open table practice of Jesus would inform the table practice of these communities.

The final meal Jesus shared with His disciples—His last supper—is this meal that Christ followers travel back to in the Spirit when they partake of the Lord's Supper, of the bread and wine. It is this meal that portends the meal that is yet to come in the marriage supper of the Lamb. And it is this meal that both Peter, who is about to deny Jesus, and Judas, who is about to betray Him, are clearly invited to share in. (In the case of Judas, this is particularly clear in Luke's Gospel[5]). These two disciples would fail the One who initiated the meal almost immediately after partaking of it, yet they had a place at the table. The faithful alongside the faithless. The beloved alongside the betrayer. Those that declare the Christ alongside those who will deny Him.

Rich's life reflected this same idea. He ate with outsiders at wrong times, in wrong places. He knew both the sanctity and the scandal of sharing the Lord's table with both the faithful and the faithless.

Jesus did not die on the cross to constrict the table, but to open it even wider. It was never intended to be the table for the holy, but the table that makes us whole. In the words of Jesus Himself, "It is not those who are well that need a physician, but the sick."[6] Christ never required us to be well in order to take the medicine of His presence.

Some will insist that the table is for transformed lives, but I would insist it is the open table of the Lord that transforms lives! The act of responding to Christ's invitation—our own admission of our deep hunger and need—transforms us. Receiving the fact that He has already received us, accepting that we are accepted, transforms us. And the partaking of the bread and wine allows us to become the body of Christ broken and the blood of Christ poured out like an offering for the world—the final stage of transformation.

Christians believe that something transcendent happens through this supremely earthy practice of eating and drinking, something that allows all those who partake to become one. Like the two disciples on the road to Emmaus, who were unaware of who Jesus was until they ate at the table, our eyes, too, are opened to see God in the breaking of bread by human hands. Through the eating of this bread and drinking of this cup, we do not judge each other, but recognize Christ, and one another.

———

And he took bread, gave thanks and broke it, and gave it to them, saying, "This is my body given for you; do this in remembrance of me." In the same way, after the supper he took the cup, saying, "This cup is the new covenant in my blood, which is poured out for you."

Luke 22:19–20 NIV

CHAPTER 40

BODY AND WATER

If we can admit a need, if we aren't as all-together
(as we sometimes secretly fear we're not), if we can shed our
thick-skinned self-reliance and peel off that thin veneer of
satisfaction—then there is a place for us in His kingdom and
a fairly fat chance that we can loosen our load and slip on
through. If we can find that courage . . . or that honesty . . .
if we can be needy, helpless, blessed as a child. . .

RICH MULLINS

I was six years old, going on seven, when I was baptized. Situated in a high loft behind the choir, my long-time friend, Sam, and I waded into that chilly pool at Ash Creek Baptist Church in Azle, Texas, and took the plunge. Following our divine dunk, his mom sang an Amy Grant song. Well, she attempted to sing an Amy Grant song as her voice cracked under the weight of her heart's emotion.

It wasn't magical. Yet I still find it difficult to explain. An extraordinary transformation happens when we press the burden of our bodies against the resistance of water to release each and every transgression past, present, and future beneath the baptismal tide, emerging from that christening basin, body dripping wet, soul spotless clean . . . just like new. Baptism is a mysterious thing. In a physical sense, it's just body and water. But in a very spiritual sense, it is soul and salvation—this full-bodied surrender into the resurrection of our heart and spirit.

My youngest niece, Lily, was recently baptized. During a weekend visit a few weeks prior to my niece's sacred ceremony, I attended church with my brother's family. Unbeknownst to me, Lily, who possesses a certain mischievous spunk, was readying herself to "walk the aisle" to profess her decision to follow Jesus publicly—to give the offering of her tender spirit to the Creator who has breathed His life into her from the beginning.

Out of my peripheral vision, I glimpsed her vivacious six year-old self slip out of our pew and shuffle down to the front of the auditorium. I leaned forward, maneuvering my line of vision between the people in front of me so I could witness this moment in Lily's grand story—her conversion into forever life. As her pastor leaned down to pray, Lily bowed her knees to the ground, clasped her hands together, held them to her lips and formed words that I swear must have enraptured the heavens with marvelous delight—words first formed by the lips of her Messiah, and words that have pierced the souls of generations of disciples ever since: "My Father in heaven, holy is Your name. Your kingdom come, Your will be done in my heart as it is in heaven."

We all are immersed in earthly life every single day. In a practical sense, it's just another swipe of the calendar, another twenty-four/seven in the list of days we are given. But from a bigger picture perspective, as seen through vivid spiritual eyes, each day is a renewal, a revival, an opportunity to lay to bed our past, take a deep breath in the present, and refuel the hope in our hearts for the future. Each moment offers another chance to dive headlong into the wild wave of mercy, and to resurface as brand *new*.

"The experience of drowning, through the lens of faith, is what Christians call 'baptism.' But no matter what you call it, the sensation of going under is entirely the same," writes author Jonathan Martin[7]. We all go under. But through our belief in Jesus Christ, we don't stay there. We have welcomed the birth of belief into our hearts, so no matter what our days bring—the good, the bad, the joyful, and the sorrow-filled—we will resurface. With Jesus we are raised to a new redeemed reality. Like Lily, for those of us who have, as Rich Mullins says, "shed our thick-skinned

self-reliance," we will raise our cup of Life to drink in deep
the redemption of new life, every single day . . . forever.

------

*I ritually cleanse you through baptism as a mark of
turning your life around. But someone is coming
after me, someone whose sandals I am not fit to carry,
someone who is more powerful than I. He will wash
you not in water but in fire and with the Holy Spirit.*

MATTHEW 3:11

CHAPTER 41

Reflections on Rich

Reed Arvin

Another tune forms in my head
More harmonies, more empty words.
Oh, I could play these songs 'til I was dead
And never approach the sound that I once heard.
I remember when I was just a kid, listening to the sky
Believing that the wind would stir.

Rich Mullins (from "The River")

Great poets reveal our most secret spaces with their words. Rich was marvelous at this kind of poetic songwriting. As I sat with him in the studio making music, I was continually inspired, but I didn't appreciate until years later the cost he paid to tell his stories so truly.

There's a reason so little writing illuminates the soul: it's *hard.* There is, of course, the discipline of writing, rewriting, and re-rewriting, but it also has to do with the risky business of the soul—to embark on the poet's journey is to take a ride on a wild river to an uncertain destination.

> *The river is deep, I found out that the currents are tricky . . . And I may lose every dream I dreamt that I could carry with me.*
>
> RICH MULLINS (FROM "THE RIVER")

To ask life's most difficult questions is to risk drowning in them. This fear is honorable. Without real danger, the hero's journey means nothing. We trust our heroes to go further into the wild than we dare, and if they survive, to return with wisdom from the edge. Comfortable in our sheltered lives, we then pick up a few pearls—and that's fair enough. But as we remember Rich, let us be mindful of the cost of his journey.

Rich possessed great joy, and the sound of his laughter is imprinted on my mind, but there is a price associated with possessing such an electrifying gift. Poets like Rich are never truly alone in their fragile little boats, and Rich made his life's journey with many unwanted passengers. Crowded in with him were self-recriminations of hypocrisy and inadequacy. Riding shotgun were seductions of fame and success, which he feared to the point of building walls of protection. But eventually, every true poet realizes that he sails toward his own reflection, which stares back at him. On the worst days, this figure whispers, "All your words and harmonies are empty." Rich was no stranger to this voice, and he surely wrote "The River" on such a day.

Rich was brilliant but, like most prophet-poets, haunted. Jeremiah heard the wind stir, too, and as grateful as I am for his writing, I wouldn't change places with him. But we need these souls to remind us that our own safety is mostly an illusion. We are, all of us, haunted by something. I have my ghosts; you have yours.

I miss Rich Mullins. I miss him when I see the bland, yet somehow hyper-animated, faces smiling back at me from many Christian books. I miss him when I hear the spiritual Ambien streaming from most of Christian radio. Rich wrote and lived dangerously. He has never been more relevant.

For the LORD is the one who shaped the mountains, stirs up the winds, and reveals his thoughts to mankind. He turns the light of dawn into darkness and treads on the heights of the earth.

AMOS 4:13 NLT

The prodding of my heart leads me to chase after You.
I am seeking You, Eternal One. . . .
My father and mother have deserted me,
yet the Eternal will take me in.

PSALM 27:8, 10

CHAPTER 42

ORPHAN CHILD

To pray is to accept that we are, and always will be,
wholly dependent on God for everything.

TIMOTHY KELLER

Gillian Welch is one of Nashville's most revered song-writers. Along with her jack-of-all-trades talented husband, David Rawlings, the folk singer has created an enormous following independent of mainstream record labels simply (and yet so profoundly) by ministering exquisitely sparse, plain songs rife with real life.

"Orphan Girl," a modern-day, melody-driven retake on *The Pilgrim's Progress*, is arguably Welch's most widely sung song. Whether humming the tune to myself, singing along in my car, or performing it live on stage, I often change the lyric's hook to "orphan *child*" in hopes of transferring the power of the refrain to myself, and to all people who might be listening in (how inclusive, I know).

The plaintive song traces the journey of a pilgrim who is parentless, and so, rather alone. But in her loneliness (for the sake of simplicity and to honor the lyric's original request, we'll refer to the song's subject with feminine pronouns), the subject shares her vulnerable situation with fellow pilgrims as they cross her path, before she begins to dream of the future when she will meet her family in the afterlife around "God's table."

Throughout the song, the subject repeats the vagabond statement, "I have no mother, no father, no sister, no brother," but with the final stanza she turns her perspective from her external circumstances to her inner condition and prays for God to be her mother, her father, her sister, and her brother. In essence, she asks God, alone, to become her *everything*—to be her home. Her cries chorus the same sense of loss that riddled Rich's speech and permeated his vagrant lifestyle. His songs were haunted by his search for home and a loneliness that can only be alleviated by God.

When I first heard the humble request of that final refrain, I was instantly moved by the song subject's earnest yearning for God to be more than just a provider or protector. Though I grew up in a fairly functional two-parent household, I have uttered that same prayer, and after hearing it sung I was confronted with the boldness of the language.

Growing up, the post assigned to God most often was that of "father," and on occasion, one of being our "friend." I get it. Jesus recommended we pray like Him and He began His prayers with "Our Father." Even without Jesus's scriptural endorsement, we are born with an innate desire to follow the leadership of our own fathers. To receive God's shepherding love is not a far cry from what we look to our own earthly dads to provide— guidance and practical support. However, whether through quiet implications or tacit disapproval, many of us learned to keep the more personal (yet majorly complementary) characteristics of God at bay. Virtues like comforter, nurturer, consoler, and grace-giver.

The problem with this hallowed separation is that we then gird our search with expectations of a one-dimensional God rather than the full reality of a comprehensive, and incomprehensible, Creator.

I don't know when in human history we became so uncomfortable with the overwhelming intimacy of God. One ramble through a mountain's forest, or the happenstance of a shooting star, and the notion of God as some mad scientist scoping us out as mere organisms on earth's magnificent petri dish instantly crumbles beneath the intense phenomenon of His longing to love us as sons and daughters, sibling and cohorts, to coexist with Him just as He created.

What might change in how we interact with ourselves and how we interact with others if we received the fullness of a relationship with God? What more of His vast character might we receive—more love, more power, more mercy, more humility, more grace—if we opened our minds and hearts to His inconceivable ability and eternal passion to be not only our father, but our mother, and our sister, and our brother—this covetous, insatiable desire for God to be our absolute, total, complete *everything*?

What might we discover if we relinquished our control, our pride, and our humanity to His sovereignty, His glory, and His eternity? I have a hunch we might finally surrender ourselves home.

CHAPTER 43

THE REDEMPTION OF THE DO-GOODERS

Brandon Heath

*The ragamuffin who sees his life as a voyage of discovery
and runs the risk of failure has a better feel
for faithfulness than the timid man who hides
behind the law and never finds out who he is at all.*

BRENNAN MANNING

It is important that we relate to one another. I look up to people who I feel are telling my story, either through their writing or through their songs—it makes me feel as though I am not alone. If I am on stage portraying a perfect, unbroken person, it would not only be inaccurate, it would be inauthentic. When I have an open conversation with an audience about something I am struggling with, even if it was only for that day, something ongoing, or something controversial, we can connect with each other on a heart level.

As people of faith, we struggle because we know our salvation is secure, but we also know we struggle daily with sin. We literally face life and death at all times. I think it is healthy to engage both—not to fall deeper into sin for the sake of engaging, but to be unafraid to say, "I am imperfect. I sin. This is who I am." Hopefully, this helps tell the bigger story of who we all are.

Jesus's life was always about humility, about servant-hood—which is never convenient and requires giving something, which means losing something. As a "wounded healer," Jesus knew His fate, He knew that He would be broken, and there is something powerful in the touch of a healer who can identify with us in our brokenness. He is ultimately God, but He is ultimately a man in the flesh, so Jesus carries healing in one hand and brokenness in the other.

It seems through his songs and stories, Rich was fighting against traditionalism and religiosity. Most people think that to be a Christian means to be "good," but being "good" is such an unattainable goal—what we really need is redemption. Rich was retraining his thought process and reminding us that though we will never be "good" enough, grace covers the need for goodness. We don't have to be "good," we just need to be redeemed, and understand what that means, and who we receive it from—that it is only through Jesus—that full love and grace that God extends to us that will change us from the inside out. This doesn't mean we become perfect, but someday we will be fully sanctified . . . just not yet. We are still on the road.

I want others to know that I am still on the road as well. If I have arrived where I am going, then I have nothing else to learn, and if I have nothing else to learn, then, frankly, I don't think I have anything else to offer—and it is in our offering that we connect with God, and with one another.

If we walk step by step in the light, where the Father is, then we are ultimately connected to each other through the sacrifice of Jesus His Son. His blood purifies us from all our sins. If we go around bragging, "We have no sin," then we are fooling ourselves and are strangers to the truth. But if we own up to our sins, God shows that He is faithful and just by forgiving us of our sins and purifying us from the pollution of all the bad things we have done. If we say, "We have not sinned," then we depict God as a liar and show that we have not let His word find its way into our hearts.

1 JOHN 1:7–10

Someday I shall be a great saint—like those you see in the windows of magnificent cathedrals. I will have a soul made of sunlight and skin as clear as the stained glass panels that make their skin, and I will shine like they do now—I will shine with the glory that comes over those who rise up early and seek the Lord . . . but I do not shine so now—especially in the morning.

RICH MULLINS

CHAPTER 44

The (Lonely) Road Home

*Just a few years ago that I realized friendship is not
a remedy for loneliness. Loneliness is a part of our experience,
and if we're looking for relief from loneliness in friendship,
we're only going to frustrate that friendship—that friendship,
camaraderie, intimacy, all those things and loneliness
live together in the same experience.*

RICH MULLINS

Though I was barely a teenager when Rich Mullins died, several of his songs were already fixed in my memory. The plaintive strains of "The Love of God" and "Hold Me Jesus" were buried somewhere in my soul to be called up by my wandering heart many times in the years to come.

I remember listening to a conversation Rich recorded at a local Central Texas radio station in the mid-1990s. He talked about eternal things and how he pined for a story the elements of wind and water only began to tell. Though nearly thirty years his junior, and still just a child at the time, I recognized the ache of loneliness that focused his music on heading towards home. I thought, *I know what you're talking about, Rich. I know that feeling, too.*

Loneliness is a common human denominator. It is a feeling exclusive to no one, inclusive of everyone. For those of us with a more melancholic bent (cue artistic types), loneliness is a bit more persistent. We tend to steep in it, at times awhile too long, until we percolate and pour out some creative inspiration—paintings, songs, narratives, plays, and poems—that help us and others framework the complexity of being human, yet eternal. Even for those with the cheeriest of dispositions, aloneness lingers close by.

Though being alone is one of the most fundamental realities of living, we try to keep it at bay by seeking a marriage mate. But even as we sleep shoulder to shoulder with our closest human companion, loneliness persists. Kids excel in music or in sports in hopes of being picked for the part or position, and adolescents partake in a myriad of unhealthy behaviors to fit in, to have friends, to belong. We'll go to such great lengths of mind, body, and heart to feel un-alone.

Perhaps the anxiety of being alone is so assertive because

we correspond aloneness with being unloved, and if ever the plight of humanity was summed up by a single objective, it is our desire to be loved. All the beds we made but never dreamed we would have to lie in, all the morning afters and the corresponding frustrations, general confusions, struggles with self-esteem and doubt—all develop from an attempt to be loved, to feel anything but alone.

My mother and father have been married for forty-five years and they seem to really dig each other . . . still. So in my own search for companionship amid the persisting feelings of loneliness, I asked Dad, "Do you ever feel alone?" thinking the question was void before it was ever vocalized because of the intimacy and friendship my parents have experienced in their long relationship. He said, "Son, I can be sitting right beside your mother, the person on this earth who knows me better than anyone, and feel so alone."

The fact remains, though signs of forever are blooming and blowing all around us, we are not yet home. And the prodding of loneliness that abides within us, especially when we are present enough to be aware of it, is the gracious gesture of God to get us back to Him, to get us back to where we are never alone—to get us back to home.

The True God who inhabits sacred space is a father to the fatherless, a defender of widows. He makes a home for those who are alone.

PSALM 68:5–6

CHAPTER 45

REFLECTIONS ON RICH

Ian Morgan Cron

---

*The man who fears to be alone will never be anything
but lonely, no matter how much he may surround himself
with people. But the man who learns, in solitude
and recollection, to be at peace with his own loneliness,
and to prefer its reality to the illusion
of merely natural companionship, comes to know
the invisible companionship of God.*

THOMAS MERTON

I immediately resonated with Rich's music when I first heard it in the eighties and nineties.

There were plenty of joyful, celebratory songs in Rich's catalog, but the ones I felt most drawn to were the laments that gave language to the longing of those who live in the age of the "now, but not yet." His songs made us pine for that far off country and made us feel unashamed with our disease with the world as we know it.

Victor Hugo said, "Melancholy is the happiness of being sad," and Rich could arouse that sentiment in his listeners. His music vacillated between loss and fulfillment, a kind of strident triumphalism and defeat. Through his music, he was on a quest for meaning and depth, a search for what was missing, this air of dissatisfaction and a desperate desire to connect personally with others. For me, it's what makes his music so compelling. That is why you have artists: for three minutes and thirty seconds, you get to rent their unusual worldview—their perceptive appreciation of creation, their ecstasy and anguish—and, for a moment, you don't feel alone.

I know Rich went through periods when he looked for solace in the wrong places to mute his longing for heaven. I understand. I've tried to numb that aching nostalgia for heaven as well. Like many artists, Rich was attuned and responsive to the frequencies of God in a way that most folks aren't. In his music it's clear he was keenly aware of a heavenly country that none of us have ever seen but we know exists, and where our hearts long to be. He awakened in us that same pining.

You hear a raw vulnerability in Rich's voice when he sings. He's not only singing to his audience; he's singing to himself, to God, to the few who will understand. It's an expensive proposition but it's the price of admission if you want to create good art.

The path we walk is charted by faith, not by what we see with our eyes. There is no doubt that we live with a daring passion, but in the end we prefer to be gone from this body so that we can be at home with the Lord.

2 CORINTHIANS 5:7–8

I can see, and that is why I can be happy, in what you call the dark, but which to me is golden. I can see a God-made world, not a manmade world.

Helen Keller

CHAPTER 46

SNOW DAY

The longer I live, the more I have the feeling like
God looks down, like when you've just bitten into a vanilla
ice cream cone—you just get the feeling of God going,
"Yes! He enjoys it, and I made his taste buds and I made
vanilla and he's putting it together and he's experiencing
what I created him to experience."

RICH MULLINS

Growing up in the South, where plows were employed for tilling land and chains were designed for towing trucks, a mere mention of "winter weather" could elicit sheer panic in the hearts of Dixie's warm-blooded residents. As temperatures fell blood pressures skyrocketed, and within a matter of minutes reason and logic were dismissed for "sensible" reactions like ransacking grocery stores, ditching cars in strangers' yards, and hunkering down at home for days harboring suspicions of terror and convictions of Armageddon.

Of course, there are always children to balance the scales. Utter the phrase "snow day" and kids worldwide howl with collective grade school euphoria. Taking a cue from the babes, even the most austere adolescent will exhale a sigh of relief knowing that under midwinter's frosty charity, the world's dizzying spin decelerates and the earth and all its inhabitants hibernate in a peaceful awe of winter's magnificent respite.

Snow is an enchanting little substance. Its poetic, long fall to the earth pleasures our aesthetic sensibilities—wispy ice flakes sashay from the atmosphere's frigid dome, latching on to earth's cold crust and glazing its barren ground with a fleece of spotless silver. Even with wintry weather's associated aggravations, snow provides a thrill for our sights and a tonic for our spirits.

There is a mystery in nature's quavering elements—the shift of seasons, the tumult-then-tranquil of weather—that reminds our soul of something so familiar, something so akin to home. Perhaps this is why we feel so comfortable under the canopy of the out-of-doors—why the natural order feels, well, so natural, and good, and right—because the earth and all that is in it was created with our pleasure, our happiness, in mind.

Ever since our humanness was revealed in the corruption of Eden, we have tried to surmise what emerges from the ashes of this physical life and death. *Does more life commence when this segment of life ends?* We discuss, debate, and obsess over the hereafter in an eagerness to hone in on some reality that can fulfill this perpetual longing, this inborn optimism that though "for now we only see a reflection as in a mirror,"[8] soon, surely—hopefully— we will know in full.

Some believe in a faraway land built on slabs of gold and bordered by crystal-clear waters. Others interpret Jesus's model prayer—"on earth as it is in heaven"[9]— as God's final intention in anticipation of a complete refresh and reframe of the cosmos to house God's place for eternal life. Some think it's a posture of the heart, others a state of mind, but in reality, we have little idea how this whole thing pans out.

Even so, there are hints of who we are and how we fit into the glorious mosaic of eternity. These intimations are continually unfolding before our eyes and maturing in our souls. Long before we could call out God's name or pray for His help, His infinite existence was implanted within our DNA—as if in the fibers of our very form He has whispered, "You belong. You are Mine. I love you, forever."

I have never been resuscitated from a flatline, or received some heavenly vision, or been enlightened by otherworldly details. To try to nut-and-bolt eternity feels as impossible, and unnecessary, as attempting to find the end of God. Yet we are compelled into life eternal again and again through His wild and wonderful Spirit alluring our hearts and relentlessly pursuing our souls through the endless uncovering of His goodness (like vanilla ice cream cones and snow days and grace).

God is our eternal objective, our forever landing place . . . where we are rescued and safe and loved. He is home.

For now, we can only see a dim and blurry picture of things, as when we stare into polished metal. I realize that everything I know is only part of the big picture. But one day, when Jesus arrives, *we will see clearly, face-to-face. In that day, I will fully know just as I have been wholly known* by God.

1 CORINTHIANS 13:12

CHAPTER 47

LITURGICAL LIVING

Jimmy Abegg

*This is what liturgy offers that all the razzmatazz
of our modern worship can't touch. You don't go home from
church going, "Oh I am just moved to tears." You go home
from church going, "Wow, I just took communion and you
know what? If Augustine were alive today, he would have
had it with me and maybe he is and maybe he did."*

RICH MULLINS

We are a product of what we live. One of the things that
I loved most about Rich was he was literally a product of
what he lived.

In any good story, there's a beginning, a middle, and
an end. Liturgy is profound because it paints a pattern—
it becomes a compass in a person's life. Whether daily,

weekly, or monthly, hopefully there is enough frequency that it will evoke habits that inspire the people that you are with, and it will invoke personal traits that are more like the fruit of the Spirit.

Agitators could say liturgy is just the church inventing a way to keep everybody under control. I have heard people argue that with great ability, and they might win the debate with me, but the same could be said for the Stations of the Cross, which is a historic invention to inspire faithfulness and regularity among Christians—to not just practice their faith, but to come to church and *do* the Stations of the Cross. It is a physical evidence of something that's supposed to be taking place internally.

To me, the liturgy is just fundamental instructional ideas. You don't have to follow it—there are people who love to walk barefooted in the snow. There are people that love to go in the rain without a raincoat. There are many ways to live, but the liturgy can function as a kind of baseline for living as a believer. If we can subscribe to even a small portion of it, liturgy brings something unnoticed to light in your inner life. The way I understand and practice the liturgy is to remind myself of what it must be like to be saintly, or to be humble, or to be meek, or to be righteous.

In my stronger Catholic days, I went to mass every day. The beauty of attending any kind of denomination that expresses its worship through a tried and true liturgical year—if you and I live in different parts of the world, you live in Calcutta and I live in Colorado, through the liturgy we hear a similar message in our daily life. We are unified. If we could execute some level of liturgy in our existence as a community, wouldn't life be different? It's an unattainable goal, but if we don't aim high, how can we hit higher?

What I have come to discover, what Rich helped me discover, is the things that are most important in life are invisible, like the idea of friendship. What is real friendship? Well, real friendship is that you would lay down your life for another. That's strong. I can't even get my mind around that.

This is part of why I believe that liturgical living can create in us the kind of atmosphere that can be contagious for spiritual evolvement and for birth and rebirth of all kinds. It is heaven. If we practice a routine, a silent pursuit of a God who cares for us, then we will find Him. Knock and the door will be opened. These are simple concepts and I don't think it is that hard to be semi-obedient where they are concerned.

Liturgy is a life-changing mechanism in the world for our benefit. It helps define the highway for living. I'm still on that highway.

The wisdom that comes from heaven is first of all pure; then peace-loving, considerate, submissive, full of mercy and good fruit, impartial and sincere.

JAMES 3:17 NIV

CHAPTER 48

A Conversation
with Mike Blanton,
Don Donahue,
and Randy Cox

In part, Rich's music influenced so many people because it was heard by so many people. Mike Blanton, Don Donahue, and Randy Cox are the core of a wider circle of music industry professionals who thoughtfully and diligently aided Rich in making his music accessible for the greater good. Their heart for music, for Rich, and for God is evident.

Q: Mike, you were among Rich's first influences in Nashville and in the record-making process. How did you first encounter the music of Rich Mullins?

Mike Blanton: I was attending a Christian music event at Nashville Shores. I was the A&R part of Reunion Records at that time and part of Blanton & Harrell, my management team with Dan Harrell. As would often happen, this girl came up to me and said, "Are you Michael Blanton? I have something to give you," and she handed me a cassette tape.

The girl was Elizabeth Lutz, and she had been in a band with Rich called Zion while they were attending Cincinnati Bible College. Her longtime friend, Kathy Sprinkle (also of CBC), was with her. They were huge advocates for Rich. The cassette featured Rich and his song "Sing Your Praise to the Lord." The song was this long, ten-minute thing, but it was magnificent.

Dan Harrell and I were establishing Amy as a Christian artist, and I thought, *This would be a huge song for Amy.* I played the song for Amy and her long-time producer, Brown Bannister. We all flipped out over the song. I called Rich and told him Amy wanted to record it—he was tremendously excited—and I asked him why the song was so long. His way of answering was so unvarnished and refreshing, I thought, *I have to meet this guy.*

We invited him to Nashville and signed him to a publishing deal with Randy at Meadowgreen Music Company.

Q: What did you first hear in Rich's songs that intrigued you—where you thought, *I want to see where this goes?*

Randy Cox: Meadowgreen was in the building of what is now Sony Music Publishing. My office was in a corner and I had a piano in it. Rich was one of the quirkiest individuals I had ever met. He would come in, sit down at the piano, cross his leg, never used the soft pedal, and he always played fortissimo—he rocked the walls.

Outside of my office sat the bookkeepers, key accountants, and everyone else. After he left, they would come to me in private and ask, "Could you soften him down? He's driving us crazy!" But after about a month or so, they would knock on my door when Rich was playing and say, "Can we stand here and listen?" That was what I saw in him—this dynamic person who was so gifted, and a bit lost.

Q: How did you guys help shape Rich's ideas, musically and lyrically, into songs that might have a chance at being heard in a commercial music landscape?

Randy: In virtually every song he ever wrote, there was a musical motif—heavy left-hand, heavy bass. He would sit down at the piano, play a music lick, then another motif, then another lick, and say, "What do you think?" I'd reply, "Pick one!"

As a song publisher, I feel like my job is to discern where a writer is currently and give direction and encouragement to build on their strengths and help their weaknesses. I had never worked with anybody like Rich. We would work through his ideas and I could see him start to pare down from three ideas in every song to one idea. He was still at the early stage of exploring the depth of his lyrics and the broadness of where his songs would take him.

Mike: Most people in the early CCM market didn't know what to do with Rich. He was an oddity, he smelled like he'd been smoking twenty packs a day, he was barefoot, he had the weirdest stories every time he'd come in town, but when he'd hand us those cassettes with those songs they would be really incredible. Early on, I realized Rich was so raw as an artist and in his methodology of making music that he needed a counter, a ying to his countrified, don't wanna be too dressed up, leave me in my overalls, barefooted look. So I paired Rich with Reed Arvin, who was also a keyboardist for Amy Grant at the time, to produce his records. Reed was a brilliant musician. He was incredibly intellectual. In my head, the blend would be great, and it started out really well . . .

Don Donahue: . . . but Reed was a North Texas music school graduate, orchestra conductor, and Rich is a barefooted, left-handed guitar player—at some point it's going to clash. And it sometimes did.

Q: Now, thirty years later, we know and understand Rich through this "ragamuffin" lens, of someone who was willing to buck the system for the sake of discovering God authentically. When and how did this ragamuffin theme become his focus?

Don: Rich was incredibly generous and loyal as a friend, so I think he just wanted to take care of his band. The Ragamuffins truly had good chemistry, but it was more their brokenness of human spirit and love of God that connected them—and that's why I identified with them. I wasn't raised in the church. I didn't know the Bible like Rich. He was clearly a scholar of the Bible without the religious trappings. He never understood why he had to hide when he would smoke a cigarette at intermission. I thought, *This is fascinating. How do you write these biblically based songs and then live this "out there" lifestyle?* The last years of his life he lived on an Indian reservation in a hogan and was hard to reach.

Mike: Until he wrote "Awesome God," I tried to hold him in the lanes of a commercially viable artist while maintaining some kind of "Rich" integrity, but he was starting to separate himself with this barefoot, "ragamuffin" thing, and he was starting to take off with subgroups on the fringes of the Christian market. That was just not in my wheelhouse. He became this theologian out there on the road. He would sit and talk and play. We had solidified him in the market as a phenomenal singer-songwriter so there was enough music to give him leeway to become his own ragamuffin guy.

Q: These between-songs conversations, it seems this is what really began to establish Rich's listening audience.

Don: He wasn't musically sensational. You attended a show to see what he was going to say. No matter what happened that afternoon on the drive, it was going to come out somehow. That's what his audience really cared about. Almost everything he was speaking to the church about are topics that we are now wrestling with. Twenty-five years ago, he was talking about things that the United States' presidential election was wrestling with just last year. Believers are fractioned because of politics. *How do you love people that don't have the same lifestyle as you? Is the goal of your life a cushy, middle-class, white, suburban life?* These questions drew ragamuffin types to him.

Rich's writing made God so approachable. He wrote about the humanness of God. I never thought, *I don't trust this guy's faith.*

Randy: There was certainly a depth in his lyrics—he was reading and studying and praying and learning and seeking and digging deeper roots. As his lyrics developed, you saw how profound his faith was. He was able to extract truth from the Word, from things he heard, from things he saw and learned—with all the baggage that comes with our living—and all of that came together in his writing.

One of the greatest things I have ever heard said of me was during a Gospel Music Association panel. Rich answered one of the questions and said, "Randy taught me how to write songs." I remember that moment.

He was the kind of person that I can certainly see in the lives of ancient saints. . . . He did leave a legacy of great, profound poetry.

Q: In a television interview in 1992, Rich said, "Nothing can be more important than becoming fully who you are supposed to be. For me, that is what salvation is all about." Considering your relationship with Rich, does that resonate?

Don: I think about the many pivots he made personally—he moved to Nashville and loved that for a season. He was angry Nashville didn't have enough bicycle trails, so he moved to Wichita where they had great bike trails. In Wichita he became fascinated with the Native American culture. That's where "Calling Out Your Name" and "The Color Green," those epic nature songs, were written. Then he tired of Kansas and moved to New Mexico to serve the poor. He couldn't have lived my life—get married in your midtwenties, have kids, and live in the suburbs—that wasn't what he liked.

This is tough to say, but getting hit by a truck was probably the way he was supposed to die. It was a kind of metaphor for how crazy his life was—he was taking chances all of the time. He was one of the most restless people I knew, but in that restlessness he was trying to figure out who he was in life . . . fully who he was. I don't think he settled on or was comfortable with who God made him . . . like all of us . . . and that's why I was so drawn to him . . . his authenticity.

Mike: Rich was reaching for something that was truly spectacular. He had a visual of God lyrically that was touching the hem of the Lord's garment. Salvation is being what God has called us to be, but the vision of who we are is so much bigger than what we even allow ourselves to think about.

Q: The portion of "The Lord's Prayer" in Matthew 6 that traditionally reads, "Give us this day our daily bread," is translated as, "Give us each day that day's bread—*no more, no less*"[10] in The Voice. If you consider the way Rich lived his life, those words feel like a "Rich" translation. But the reality of those words are difficult living within a culture that constantly opts to prepare for the future over being present in the here and now.

Don: I do believe it's noisier than ever, harder than ever to keep that simple prayer of, "Give us this day. . . ." I can't stop checking my phone. The discipline of starting the day in Scripture is not one I have consistently had in my life—to be reminded that it is daily bread.

Rich would say, and I'm paraphrasing, "I would rather

live completely on the edge, grasping for God's love and mercy, than [live] a pious life of perfectness." I always liked that person who lived out there a little bit—I wish I were a little edgier than I actually am. I wish I had Rich's ability to detach from the things of this world. It's expensive to have a family of seven with four kids in college at the same time. I whisper a prayer every morning, "I can't get through this without You." Rich knew the Word inside and out, but I don't know he had the peace of it. I don't attribute peace to Rich—pursuit, yes, but not peace.

Mike: But he knew the Father. This was a man who in the midst of his wildness, of his crazy life, had this relationship with the Father that made us think, *I want that.*

When he came in with the lyrics, "Our God is an awesome God," that was not a current saying—that was this other dimension of a loving and smiling Father that we had not thought about. Theologians would try to teach us, but Rich phrased it in a way where we understood it. Rich knew the Father was smiling and it wasn't about how good he was, it was about the position he was in with the Father.

Don: And he had the pursuit of Flannery O'Connor's prose. So that's where these wacky verses come in. He loved that imagery of God.

Q: How was that imagery an extension of his relationship with God?

Randy: When you're on a pilgrimage, you're lost, and then you find your way, and then you're lost, and then you find your way. In his early years, he was searching for a deeper faith, a deeper relationship with God, and a deeper way of expressing it that became more poetic and more powerful through the years. He was developing spiritually, but it was internal. You didn't look at Rich and think, *He's a saint!* He was anything but a saint, and everyone knew it, and everyone loved him.

There is a tangible holiness in his songs. After all these years, working with thousands of songs and hundreds of writers, I will listen to Rich's songs and weep. He changed the contemporary Christian music business in ways that will always be affecting people's lives.

Q: Part of that "tangible holiness" was how Rich was unafraid to speak and sing of brokenness. From the perspective of a listener, this was how I identified with Rich—he didn't disguise the chaos, but often displayed it. To be honest about brokenness is powerful.

Don: Everyone is broken . . . that's an essential component of the gospel. We need a Savior, but somehow we have been conditioned to think we are not broken because "Jesus loves me" and "I have accepted Christ as my Savior." So when chaos comes in your life, you think, *I'm not doing this right.* Rich felt like that's where God meets us—

when you're not doing it right, or when you are in a deep, dark valley, that's where His love lives. Chaos is a connecting tissue in Christianity that most Christians tamp down.

Q: Do you think we diminish it because we fear that God is unable to deal with it?

Don: If you look in the Gospels, there is never a threat of Him kicking us out. Certainly in the Psalms there is shaking of fists, but the New Testament is God building a bridge for us. I just don't think we want our friends to know who we are. It must be a human condition to want to have it all together.

Mike: Brokenness allows the light to shine through. When you're broken, you receive better than when you're buttoned up. Rich found comfort in being broken because he was able to receive favor and love from the Father when he was broken. Even in my life, when I am broken in my back bedroom on the closet floor weeping, and He says, "I love you," that's when I receive grace.

Rich's brokenness, his chaos, was him receiving everything the Father had to give. Until you get to the place where you have nothing left, it doesn't make sense.

Don: I don't think He was necessarily done with Rich. I miss what might have become.

Top: The Brother's Keeper tour with Carolyn Arends, 1995.
Bottom: On tour with Mitch McVicker, 1995.

AFTERWORD

Andrew Greer

For many of us who grew up attending church, the story we heard most centered on Jesus's life on earth. Abbreviated by an unjustified criminal's crucifixion at the age of thirty-three, His earthen existence culminated in the resurrection of His body from the grave three days later and the redemption of our souls forever. This glorious drama is the apex of our spiritual experience and the crux of our belief as Christians.

But it wasn't this grand gesture of grace that first compelled me to pick up my cross and follow Jesus. It was the stories He shared so personally with people—the profound parables He narrated from lakeshores and mountainsides, all of the table talks He conducted over dinner with everyday folks—people like you and me—that first tugged on my heart and spoke to my soul. Though the concepts He rendered were difficult to fully comprehend, the everyday language of His exchanges led me to believe that everyone was invited to the table of God—not simply to learn *from* Him, but to experience the deep mystery of communion *with* Him.

This was the tremendous gift of Rich Mullins's life and lyrics. No matter the topic, no matter the person, his words, spoken and sung to us decades ago, prompted conversations within our churches, our communities, and our relationships with one another that are still so obviously relevant today. His approachable prose within each verse and chorus welcomes every person to the table of God, into communion with God, regardless of heritage, lifestyle, experience with faith, or expression of doubt.

May the dialogue discerned throughout these pages continue to open your mind, soften your heart, and set your soul aflame with the never-ending conversation of eternity—that you are loved by God, not for anything you have done, or anyone you could become, but simply as the beautifully broken ragamuffin you are.

In concert, South Bend, Indiana, 1988.

The Amy Grant Unguarded Encore Tour, 1986.

THE JOY OF JESUS

May the grace of my God be with you
May the grace of my God be with you
May you know the grace of my God
And may the grace of my God be with you
May the love of my Lord be with you
May the love of my Lord be with you
May you know the love of my Lord
And may the love of my Lord be with you
And may you dance and laugh and sing
May you know the warmth of His embrace
May you feel the brush of angel wings
Like the wind upon your face
May the joy of Jesus be with you
May the joy of Jesus be with you
May you know the joy of Jesus
And may the joy of Jesus be with you . . .

RICH MULLINS, PHIL NAISH, AND LOWELL ALEXANDER[1]

Keith Bordeaux, Rich, and Jim Dunning (Rich's business manager) hiking in Canyon de Chelly, September 1997.

ACKNOWLEDGMENTS

Andrew Greer

So many people were inspired by Rich Mullins. The sheer number of delightful individuals offering me companionship as I researched his life threatened to overwhelm the progress of the project. But each artist, author, colleague, and family member's contribution to these conversations created in me more gratitude than pen and paper can muster here. The first effort of thanks must go to each of them for their generosity of spirit and beautiful recollections of Rich.

The ink on these pages would never have dried had it not been for the generous infrastructure of Worthy Publishing and the prod of Pamela Clements and her exceedingly kind staff—especially the editorial expertise of Marilyn Jansen, creative excitement of Melissa Reagan, and the marketing prowess of Cat Hoort, plus the word-by-word transcriptions from Hannah Lamb. They, like so many of us, have greatly benefitted from the impression of Rich's life and lyrics in their own lives. Thank you, ladies.

The recording of these inspirations would not exist in the first place if it had not been for Randy Cox understanding the importance of continuing Rich's life contributions and initiating this project. And to Danya Clairmont, who put my writer's pen back on paper through, of all things, social media.

Kindhearted conversations with Mike Blanton and Don Donahue, two distinctive influences on Rich's career, and therefore his legacy, gifted me with the context to better chart the focus of this book. Likewise, Jimmy Abegg filled gaps in my timeline and deepened my understanding of portions of Rich's life, as did Keith Bordeaux, who lent me his ear on several occasions as I pieced together the mosaic of Rich's relationships, which includes the very personal impact Rich had on Keith's life and work.

Dave Mullins, Rich's youngest brother, gifted me the confidence to soldier on with the offering of his voice and blessing on this project.

The earthy articulations and magnificent recollections (and photos!) from Amy Grant set these conversations into motion. Like Rich, she is truly one-of-a-kind.

The houses and homes of my cousins, Tim and Kimberly Girard, my friends, Stu and Denise Jones, Dale Houtkooper and Jackie Jones, and my parents, Tim and Jane Greer, provided a safe space for me to check out and dig into the formation of these words. Their no-strings-attached kindnesses are not lost on me. Neither is the support and determination of my manager, Rebecca Jones.

Lastly, I am indebted to my friends David McCracken and Marita Meinerts Albinson, whose very personal bond with Rich gave me a glimpse into the care and concern God provides in each of our lives through relationships with others. Their relationships with Rich have made the most impact on my relationship with this book.

ACKNOWLEDGMENTS

Randy Cox

With thanks to my late father, Johnny Cox, for giving me a love for church music.

My mom, Glenda. She is my rock.

Paul Ferrin, my first mentor.

J. Randy Smith, Esq., lifetime friend and my entryway to music publishing.

Bob MacKenzie, Wayne Erickson, and Bill Gaither, for giving me a chance.

Gary Chapman ("Father's Eyes"), my first writer.

Joe Human, my partner and friend at Meadowgreen Music.

My wife, Gloria, who gave up so much to give me so much.

Kathy Sprinkle, Liz Lutz, keeper of Rich's legacy, and members of his band, Zion.

Geoff Thurman, member of Zion and exclusive writer at Meadowgreen Music.

Mike Blanton, copublisher of Rich's songs with us at Meadowgreen. Cofounder of Reunion Records.

Amy Grant, for recording "Sing Your Praise to the Lord" and so many other songs.

David Mullins, thank you for giving me responsibility for the new, unheard eleven songs.

Lowell Alexander, my songwriter and friend since Rich brought him to me. A great lyricist and musician who finished the new songs.

Phil Naish, great player, writer, arranger who helped finish the new songs.

Craig Adams and Mike Harland for including me in Lifeway's music publishing division.

Br. Paul Quenon.

Sr. Mary Madeline.

Worthy's team: Pamela, Cat, Melissa, Marilyn, and Byron.

Andrew Greer, the hardest working man in show business!

My Lord and my God who always keeps His word!

About the Contributors

Amy Grant is a multiple Grammy Award–winning singer and songwriter. A Nashville native, she is as well known for her philanthropic efforts as she is her legendary music. Attributed with bringing Contemporary Christian Music to the forefront of American culture, Amy has gained a reputation for creating potent songs that examine life's complexities with an open heart and a keen eye.

amygrant.com

Andrew Peterson is one of gospel music's most astute artists. His record and songwriting career has yielded consistent critical acclaim, multiple Dove Award nominations, Top 10 sales status, and the Behold the Lamb of God Christmas tour, hosting sold-out performances across the country. He is also an author of the award-winning The Wingfeather Saga series. He and his family live on The Warren outside of Nashville, Tennessee.

andrewpeterson.com

Ashley Cleveland is a three-time Grammy and two-time Dove Award–winning singer, songwriter, and author.

Her powerful memoir, *Little Black Sheep*, reminds readers that even in the lowest times of our lives, beauty can shine through. Ashley and her husband, musician Kenny Greenberg, live in Nashville, Tennessee.

ashleycleveland.com

Brandon Heath is one of Christian music's most beloved and respected artists and songwriters. Having been awarded an Emmy Award, multiple Grammy nominations, and six Dove Awards, his potent songs reflect a soaring radio career, with multiple chart-toppers and a thoughtful heart for God and people. Brandon and his wife, Siebe, reside in Nashville.

brandonheath.net

The late **Brennan Manning** was known to legions of faithful readers as author, speaker, and contemplative, for whom grace was irresistible. He completed his earthly journey on April 12, 2013. He is now resting safely in the arms of his Abba. He is best known for his bestselling books, *The Ragamuffin Gospel, Abba's Child*, and his memoir, *All Is Grace*.

brennanmanning.com

As a singer, songwriter, and author, **Carolyn Arends** has released twelve albums, spawning fifteen Top 10 singles and earning two Dove Awards. Her trio of critically acclaimed books has been recognized by The Word Guild, The Evangelical Press Association, and The Canadian Church Press Awards. Carolyn is currently the director of education for Renovaré, an organization that encourages and nurtures personal and spiritual renewal. She lives in Surrey, British Columbia, with her husband, Mark, and their children, Benjamin and Bethany.

carolynarends.com

Cindy Morgan is one of Nashville's most influential singer-songwriters. For more than twenty years her prolific songs—poetically mining the depths of life, love, loss, and everything in between—have grown deep roots with listeners across the world. A two-time Grammy nominee and thirteen-time Dove Award winner for her music, she is also an author. Her latest book, *How Could I Ask for More: Stories of Blessings, Battles, and Beauty*, released in 2015.

cindymorganmusic.com

Dan Haseltine is a member of **Jars of Clay**. In the twenty years since they released their debut album, *Frail*, the humanitarian-focused band has sold millions of albums and received multiple Grammy, American Music, and Dove Awards, and major television and film song placements. Over ten years ago, the band founded Blood:Water

Mission, partnering with Africa to end the HIV/AIDS and water crises.

jarsofclay.com, bloodwater.org

David Leo Schultz is a filmmaker best known for his movies *Ragamuffin* and *Brennan*. He is also a husband, father, actor, comedian, screenwriter, and vagabond evangelist. His film production company, Color Green Films, has produced five full-length feature films to date. He also leads an annual Ragamuffin Camp, inspired by the life and legacy of Rich Mullins.

davidleoschultz.com, colorgreenfilms.com

David McCracken is a native Tennessean who spent much of his career working alongside Rich both at Reunion Records and later as assistant editor of *Release Music Magazine*. His experiences in Christian music left him well prepared to keep the "mad men" and women of one of Nashville's largest ad agencies in line for the past fifteen years. He is most passionate about spending time with those he loves, his recreational softball team, and his involvement in various men's and retreat ministries.

David Mullins is a speaker, teacher, writer, musician, and coproducer of the movie *Ragamuffin*. David seeks to use his gifts to reach those who believe they are unlovable and unworthy of God's love with the Truth. He is Rich's youngest brother and resides with his family in Florida. *kidbrothers.org*

Don Donahue is the CEO and founder of Donahue Entertainment in Nashville, Tennessee. A twenty-year veteran of the music industry, Donahue launched the boutique artist label Rocketown Records in 1996, selling more than six million albums. Donahue Entertainment joined forces with Be Music & Entertainment in 2012, where Don serves as vice president of Live Events and Program Development. Don and his family live in Franklin, Tennessee.
donahueentertainment.com

Ian Morgan Cron is a bestselling author, Enneagram teacher, nationally recognized speaker, psychotherapist, and Episcopal priest. His books include the novel *Chasing Francis,* the spiritual memoir *Jesus, My Father, the CIA, and Me,* and the Enneagram-inspired *The Road Back to You.* Ian draws on an array of disciplines to help people enter more deeply into conversation with God. He and his wife, Anne, live in Nashville, Tennessee.

After a successful independent music career, singer-songwriter **Jason Gray** signed with Centricity Music in 2006, spawning six critically acclaimed studio records, multiple ASCAP music awards, Top 5 radio singles, and a Number One song for nine consecutive weeks. His latest recording, *Where the Light Gets In*, offers a hope-centered travelogue that purports God's redemptive presence is at work even in the midst of difficulties.

jasongraymusic.com

Jimmy Abegg (Jimmy A) is an artist in every sense of the word. A guitarist, composer, photographer, video director, and painter, Jimmy's musicianship and visual artistry has been featured on a Who's Who of projects over the past quarter-century. An alumnus of Rich's all-star Ragamuffin Band, Jimmy is also an accomplished video director whose long-running relationship with director/artist Steve Taylor and photographer Ben Pearson has resulted in videos for the likes of Sixpence None the Richer, Fleming & John, and Rich Mullins. Despite the loss of his sight from macular degeneration, Jimmy continues to make art to pique the senses near his and his family's home in Nashville, Tennessee.

jimmyabegg.com

Jonathan Martin is the author of *How to Survive a Shipwreck* and *Prototype*. Hailing from the Christ-haunted landscape of the American South, Jonathan now resides in Tulsa, Oklahoma. He has a BA from Gardner-Webb University, an MA from the Pentecostal Theological Seminary, and a ThM from Duke University. Jonathan traffics in words full-time, writing and speaking about the things that move him most—God, beauty, wonder, love, loss, and all the aching things that make us human. *jonathanmartinwords.com*

Josh Blakesley has acknowledged a simple calling—to make music that moves people into prayer and action. Josh has performed and led worship for thousands of listeners, regularly partnering with Life Teen International, Catholic Heart Work Camps, and Adore Ministries, as well as churches, camps, and events across the nation. He lives in Alexandria, Louisiana, with his wife and two children. *joshblakesleyband.com*

Keith Bordeaux has helped release thousands of children from poverty in Jesus's name through his nearly twenty-year tenure at Compassion International, currently acting as the organization's senior regional director of event marketing. Through his friendship with Rich Mullins, Keith was a part of the Kid Brothers of St. Frank's ministry to Native Americans when Rich died. He and his wife, Bethany, live in the heart of Nashville, Tennessee. *compassion.com*

Lowell Alexander became one of the most prolific song-writers on Nashville's Music Row in the 1990s and early 2000s with over five hundred songs published, eighteen gold and platinum records earned, and ten Number One songs to his credit. Lowell holds a Bachelor of Arts degree from Georgia State University in Atlanta. He currently lives just outside of Nashville in Murfreesboro, Tennessee.

Marita Meinerts Albinson is a marketing and communications executive specializing in nonprofits, the arts, higher education, and small business. Music, theater, and visual arts are the languages of her soul, and she invests her time creating and promoting the arts. Marita and her sweet and wonderfully goofy husband, Jim, live outside of Minneapolis. A longtime friend of Rich's, Marita worked alongside Mullins until his death in 1997.

momentummanagementmn.com

Mark Lee and **Third Day** celebrate a powerful and uplifting twenty years since the original independent release of the band's gold-selling self-titled debut album. Lauded by *Billboard* as "one of the best rock bands, period," the band's extraordinary stats and accolades include dozens of Number One singles, nearly nine million records sold, multiple Grammy and Dove Awards, and induction into the Georgia Music Hall of Fame. The band continues to focus on the spirit of worship, a pure consistency that has inspired its loyal fans to draw closer to God.

Mark Lowry is a singer, storyteller, humorist, and song-writer whose lyrics to "Mary, Did You Know?" resulted in one of the most loved modern Christmas songs of this century. A Grammy Award winner, his long list of recordings and platinum-selling videos demonstrates his broad musicianship, deep-thinker theology, and smart comedic sensibility. A native Texan, Mark resides in Houston. *marklowry.com*

As a young adult, **Melissa Reagan** was deeply impacted by the life and music of Rich Mullins. He inspired her to pursue God with all her heart and to live truthfully, loving people in the beauty of their brokenness and imperfections. She has served on the mission field from Israel to India and would like to be a biblical archaeologist when she grows up. Until then, she is quite content living in Tennessee and playing at being creative director for Worthy Publishing.

Michael Blanton is a veteran music industry executive responsible for directing the careers of artists such as Amy Grant, Michael W. Smith, Melinda Doolittle, the late Rich Mullins, and author Frank Peretti. In 2011 he and his daughter, Chelsea Drimmel, founded Be Music

& Entertainment, where he continues to work with a diverse roster of artists. In 2017, along with Dan Harrell, he was inducted into the Gospel Music Association Hall of Fame for historic achievements, including the creation of Reunion Records over thirty years ago. His music business tenure has earned multiple platinum and gold records, and Grammy and Dove Awards. Blanton and his wife, Paula, have three children and three grandchildren. They make their home in Brentwood, Tennessee.

bemusicentertainment.com

Mitch McVicker performed hundreds of concerts with the late Rich Mullins. Mitch was in the car wreck that claimed Rich's life. While still recovering from the effects of the crash, he won the Gospel Music Association's Dove Award for "Song of the Year" with Mullins, posthumously, for the song they cowrote, "My Deliverer." He has since released numerous recordings and performed hundreds of concerts across the country. He and his family make their home in Atlanta, Georgia.

mitchmcvicker.com

Reed Arvin was Rich Mullins's long-time producer. Together they created some of Christian music's most compelling music. Reed has published four novels and is currently adjunct professor of creativity at Lipscomb

University in Nashville, Tennessee, and assists Fortune 500 companies in workplace creativity.

reedarvin.com

Sara Groves is a mom, wife, singer-songwriter, and recording artist with a passion for justice and a heart of mercy, having joined forces with International Justice Mission to advocate for victims of human trafficking for the past eight years. Nominated for seven Dove Awards, Sara, her husband, Troy, and their three children reside in St. Paul, Minnesota, where they cultivate an artist support community out of a one-hundred-year-old church called Art House North.

Sarah Hart is a Grammy-nominated singer-songwriting lover of music and the written word, a mother, a wife, daughter, friend, and clueless wonderer living in Nashville, Tennessee. Her soft-spoken musical recordings, steeped in her Catholic heritage, have gifted her with a platform for thousands of listeners, including Pope Francis. Her songs have been recorded by a wide array of artists, including Amy Grant, Celtic Woman, and Matt Maher.

sarahhart.com

Shane Claiborne is a prominent speaker, activist, and best-selling author. He worked with Mother Teresa in Calcutta, and founded of The Simple Way intentional community in Philadelphia. He heads up Red Letter Christians, a movement of folks who are committed to living "as if Jesus meant the things He said." His books include *The Irresistible Revolution, Jesus for President,* and most recently, *Executing Grace.* His work has appeared in *Esquire,* SPIN, *Christianity Today,* and the *Wall Street Journal.* Shane speaks regularly at denominational gatherings, festivals, and conferences around the globe.

shaneclaiborne.com

Notes

1. "If I Stand," Copyright © 1995 Universal Music—Brentwood Benson Publishing (ASCAP) (adm. At CapitolCMGPUblishing. com). All rights reserved. Used by permission.
2. Matthew 25:40.
3. © 2017 Goodreads Inc. http://www.goodreads.com/quotes /431738-i-am-thinking-now-of-old-moses-sitting-on-a.

Part 1

1. Excerpt(s) from THE WORLD AS I REMEMBER IT: THROUGH THE EYES OF A RAGAMUFFIN by Rich Mullins, copyright © 2004 by Old Hickory Media Group. Used by permission of WaterBrook/Multnomah, an imprint of the Crown Publishing Group, a division of Penguin Random House LLC. All rights reserved. Pages 34–35.
2. This is an unpublished song written by Rich, and completed by Phil Naish and Lowell Alexander after Mullins's death in hopes of sharing his poetic pen with many generations to come. © 2017 Mullinsongs/ASCAP (Admin. by The Loving Company), 716 Music Publishing/ASCAP (Admin. by Carlson Music Management, Inc.) and Freddie Carter Music Publishing/ASCAP (Admin. by Carlson Music Management, Inc.).
3. From "Ragamuffin" conversation tapes with director David Leo Schultz. Used with permission.
4. 1 Samuel 18:1.
5. Copyright © 1995 Universal Music—Brentwood Benson Publishing (ASCAP) (adm. At CapitolCMGPUblishing.com). All rights reserved. Used by permission.
6. Rich Mullins, Interview at close of A Ragamuffin's Legacy Documentary, used by permission.
7. Rich Mullins, Sheila Walsh Heart to Heart Interview, 1992, 18:30.

8. Acts 9.
9. John 20:29 NIV.
10. Romans 8:1 NIV.
11. Brennan Manning Live at Woodcrest, https://youtu.be/pQi_IDV2bgM.

Part 2

1. © 2017 Goodreads Inc. https://www.goodreads.com/author/quotes/139433.Rich_Mullins.
2. This is an unpublished song written by Rich, and completed by Phil Naish and Lowell Alexander after Mullins's death in hopes of sharing his poetic pen with many generations to come. © 2017 Mullinsongs/ASCAP (Admin. by The Loving Company), 716 Music Publishing/ASCAP (Admin. by Carlson Music Management, Inc.) and Freddie Carter Music Publishing/ASCAP (Admin. by Carlson Music Management, Inc.).
3. The Letters of Vincent van Gogh, Vincent van Gogh.
4. Philippians 3:2 MSG.
5. James 1:27.
6. Isaiah 53:3.
7. Rich Mullins, *The World as Best as I Remember It: Through the Eyes of a Ragamuffin* (p. 102).
8. "Growing Young," *The World As Best As I Remember It, Volume 2.*
9. ho·gan [hoh-gawn, -guh n]noun: a traditional Navajo hut of logs and earth.
10. Rich Mullins, 20 Countdown 1997 Tribute, Disc 2, Track 4, 7:45.
11. Jeremiah 20:9.
12. Rich Mullins, 20 The Countdown Magazine, 1997 Tribute, Disc 2, Track 3, 5:00.
13. Luke 1:52–53.
14. Matthew 18:20 PARAPHRASE.

Part 3

1. Rich Mullins, http://www.azquotes.com/author/32749-Rich_Mullins.

2. This is an unpublished song written by Rich, and completed by Phil Naish and Lowell Alexander after Mullins's death in hopes of sharing his poetic pen with many generations to come. © 2017 Mullinsongs/ASCAP (Admin. by The Loving Company), 716 Music Publishing/ASCAP (Admin. by Carlson Music Management, Inc.) and Freddie Carter Music Publishing/ASCAP (Admin. by Carlson Music Management, Inc.).

3. Matthew 5:4.

4. Matthew 9:11.

5. Luke 22.

6. Matthew 9:12, Mark 2:17, Luke 5:31.

7. Jonathan Martin, *How to Survive a Shipwreck* © 2017 Goodreads, Inc. https://www.goodreads.com/work/quotes/47824426-how -to-survive-a-shipwreck.

8. 1 Corinthians 13:12 NIV.

9. Matthew 6:10 NIV.

10. Matthew 6:11.

Afterword

1. This is an unpublished song written by Rich, and completed by Phil Naish and Lowell Alexander after Mullins's death in hopes of sharing his poetic pen with many generations to come. © 2017 Mullinsongs/ASCAP (Admin. by The Loving Company), 716 Music Publishing/ASCAP (Admin. by Carlson Music Management, Inc.) and Freddie Carter Music Publishing/ASCAP (Admin. by Carlson Music Management, Inc.).

Photo Credits

Photos on pages 5, 8, and 244 courtesy of Amy Grant.

Photos on pages xi, 6, 26, 84, 86, 92, 168, and 243 courtesy of David McCracken.

Photos on pages 10, 14, 88, 166, 170, and 240 courtesy of Marita Meinerts Albinson.

Photo on page 64 and 246 courtesy of Keith Bordeaux.

About the Authors

A multiple Dove Award–nominated singer/songwriter and respected author, **Andrew Greer** is known for his soulful folk-gospel sound, instinctively captured on his critically acclaimed Angel Band recordings. Andrew's 2013 hymn project, *All Things Bright & Beautiful*, held the number-one position on Nielsen Christian SoundScan's Instrumental chart for twenty-five consecutive weeks. The author of *Transcending Mysteries*, Andrew's stories have appeared in *Christianity Today, In Touch,* and *CCM*. A native Texan, Andrew makes his home in Franklin, Tennessee.

Randy Cox has nearly forty years of experience in music publishing, including his work at Paragon Music, where he discovered Michael W. Smith, and at Meadowgreen Music, where he first signed Rich Mullins. As publisher or representative, Randy's songs have been heard on more than 80 million recordings, including dozens of Grammy and Dove Award–winning albums. Randy lives in Nashville, Tennessee, where he also serves as adjunct professor at Trevecca University and a consultant with LifeWay Worship Resources.

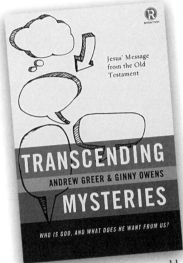

IF YOU ENJOYED THIS BOOK, WILL YOU CONSIDER SHARING THE MESSAGE WITH OTHERS?

Mention the book in a blog post or through Facebook, Twitter, Pinterest, or upload a picture through Instagram.

Recommend this book to those in your small group, book club, workplace, and classes.

Head over to facebook.com/worthypublishing, "LIKE" the page, and post a comment as to what you enjoyed the most.

Tweet "I recommend reading #WindsOfHeaven inspired by #RichMullins from @WorthyPub"

Pick up a copy for someone you know who would be challenged and encouraged by this message.

Write a book review online.

WORTHY®
P U B L I S H I N G

Visit us at worthypublishing.com

twitter.com/worthypub

worthypub.tumblr.com

facebook.com/worthypublishing

pinterest.com/worthypub

instagram.com/worthypub

youtube.com/worthypublishing